A GEOGRAPHY OF MARYLAND

ASK ME! (ABOUT MARYLAND)

Pen and ink drawings by Dinah Fiot.

Vera F. Rollo

MARYLAND HISTORICAL PRESS
9205 Tuckerman Street, Lanham, Md.

ISBN 0-917882-10-5

Library of Congress Catalog Card
No. 81-80285.
Second Printing 1984
Third Printing 1988

Printed in the United States of America.

ASK ME!
(ABOUT MARYLAND)
By
Vera Foster Rollo

MARYLAND HISTORICAL PRESS
9205 Tuckerman Street
Lanham, Maryland
20801

301-577-5308
301-577-2436

A GEOGRAPHY OF MARYLAND

TABLE OF CONTENTS

PREFACE

To make the text particularly useful in the classroom, readers of the book are constantly questioned, involved and challenged. Exercises, projects and scores of questions are designed to stimulate active participation in the learning process. The constant querying is, in fact, the reason for the title of the book, **Ask Me!**

Certainly, it is very easy to become interested and involved in our beautiful state. We rather suspect that readers of all ages will find the text stimulating and informative.

SECTION I.

MARYLAND: SIZE AND LOCATION

The Maryland State House, State House Circle, Annapolis, Maryland.

Joseph Cromwell photograph.

1. MAPS AND MILES

Direction *a line or path along which anything is moving or aimed; or along which a thing is pointing.*

Distance *how far it is from one place to another.*

Geography *a description of land, sea, air; plant and animal life; people and their work.*

Miniature *a small copy of something larger.*

Scale *the ratio of miles on the surface of the earth to the inches shown on a map. Each inch stands for a certain number of miles. A divided line marked in miles tells you how many "miles to the inch" are on a map.This is the scale of your map.*

Where in the world is Maryland? To see, look at a globe of the world. Find North America. Now find the United States of America. You will find Maryland on the east coast of the United States. (Latitude 39°N, longitude 77° W.)

On a map of the United States, locate Maryland. Because Maryland has so many kinds of land and water, our state is often called "America in Miniature." We have beaches on the Atlantic Ocean. We have flat coastal plains. The central part of our state is rolling and hilly land. Far to the west our mountains rise to more than 3000 feet above sea level. Maryland has many rivers and the beautiful Chesapeake Bay, too.

Maps Have Secrets

Maps are really pictures of places. If you know how to read them they will tell you many things. First, remember that a good map always shows you ***direction.*** On any map you will want to find the direction of North. Facing North, the East will be to the

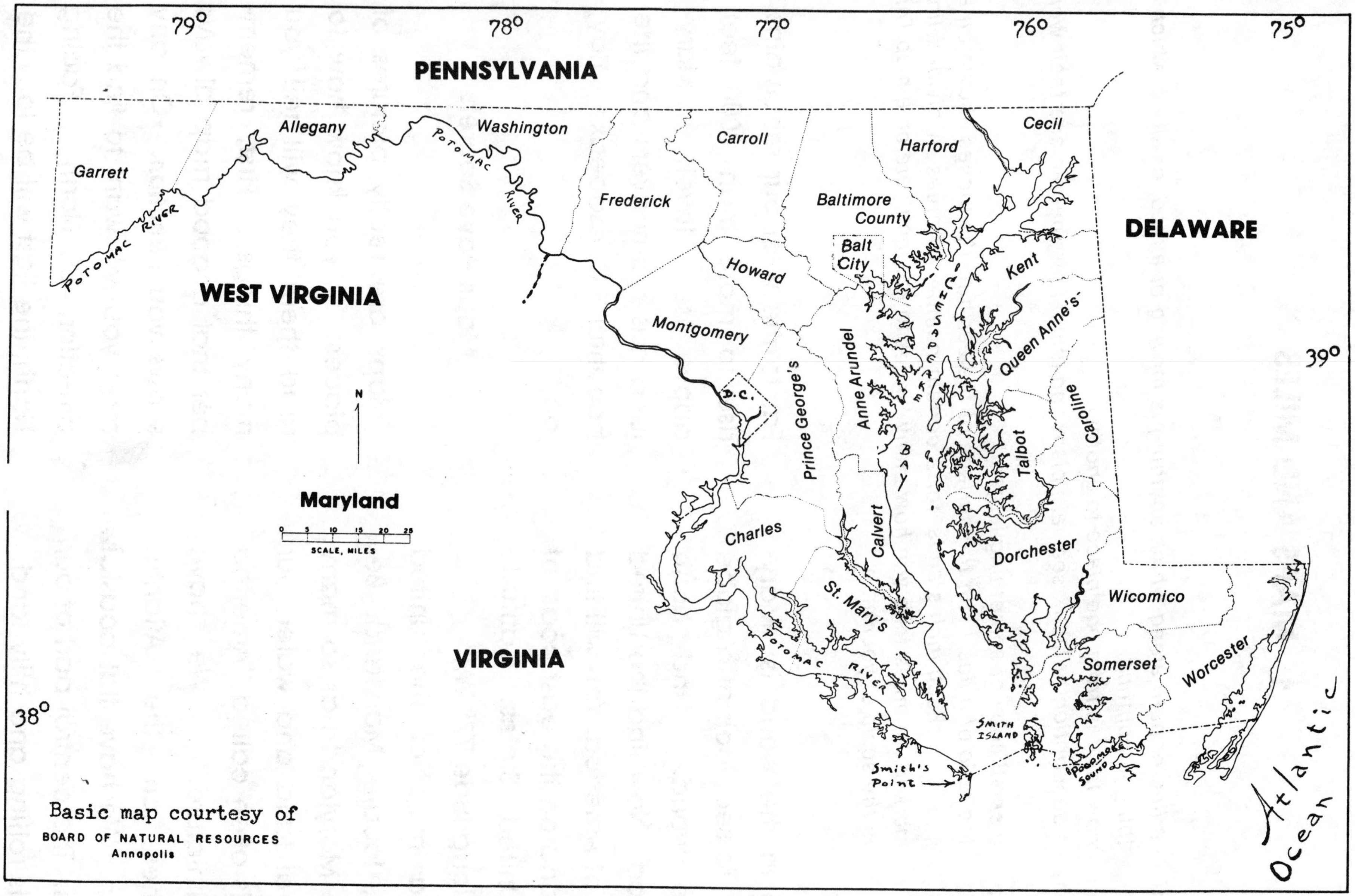

FIGURE 1. A MAP OF MARYLAND SHOWING COUNTY NAMES AND NEARBY STATES.

right, South will be behind you and West will be to your left.

Maps tell you ***distances.*** To read this from your map you must first know its "scale." Look at the map of Maryland in Figure 1. Just below the name of the state you will see a line marked "Scale, Miles." This line stands for a distance of 25 miles on this map.

EXERCISE

To measure some distances on the map in Figure 1 take a sheet of paper. Along the long side, mark 25-mile units with the scale of miles. You will be able to get eleven units on the edge of your paper. Use this to measure distances on the map and find the information needed to answer the questions below.

(1) What is the longest North-South distance in Maryland (in miles)?

(2) Measured East to West, how many miles across is our state?

(3) Maryland has a very small "waist" in Washington County. Measure it please. At this narrowest point how wide is our state?

(4) If two students wanted to see how far apart they could get but still stay in the state of Maryland, how many miles apart would they be?

A Maryland waterfront scene.

Joseph H. Cromwell photograph.

2. WHAT IS A SQUARE MILE?

Area *land or water surface amount or extent.*
Rank *an orderly arrangement of things. Standing relative to others.*

We think of a mile as a measure of length. Our statute mile, we know, is 5,280 feet long. This is the kind of mile we speak of, measuring distance from one place to another.

What is a square mile then? It is a way of measuring land or water surface ***area.*** For example:

If you tell your teacher that you would like to have a square mile of peanut butter sandwiches for lunch, you are telling her (or him) that you would like enough to cover an area a mile long and a mile wide!

A "square mile" ***can be any shape.*** It can be circular, all sides uneven, an actual square, or a parallelogram. It can be ***any*** shape. It will however have the ***same*** amount of surface enclosed.

We use the name "square miles" to tell how much area we have. A forest ranger might say that he watches 300 ***square miles*** of forest. A police officer might patrol 400 square miles of the county as he, or she, drives back and forth. An officer of the state water patrol might search 75 square miles of water area looking for a lost sailboat. We might say that a farmer owns two square miles of land. Can you think of other examples?

Old Cove Point Lighthouse, Calvert County; built in 1828.

J. H. Cromwell photograph.

You can find out how many square miles of land and water area are in Maryland by reading the following facts:

Maryland has 9,874 square miles of land area.

Maryland's Chesapeake Bay has 1,726 square miles of water area.

There are 703 square miles of inland water area in Maryland.

Maryland ranks forty-first size among all the states in the United States. There are fifty states in our nation.

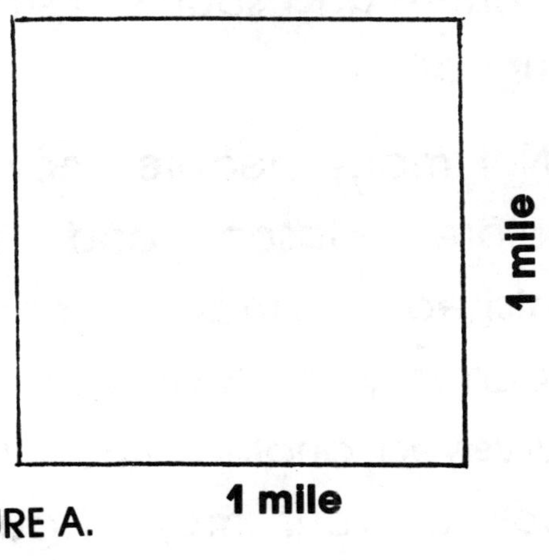

FIGURE A.

Does Maryland change in size? Yes ***and*** no! Yes, the land and water areas can change. Soil can build up, be deposited, and so build up land. Land fills, too, create new land area. This adds to land areas, subtracts from water areas. Right?

Also, land can be washed *away* along rivers, beaches, or bays---making land areas ***smaller,*** water areas larger.

The ***total area*** of Maryland, however, stays the same. We use the ***Maryland Statistical Abstract*** for the most recent measurements.

Exercise.

(1) What is Maryland's total water area in square miles?
(2) What is Maryland's total area of land and water in square miles?

(3) How many states are smaller in size than Maryland?

3. BOUNDARY "BRAIN-TWISTERS"

Astronomers *people who study stars, planets and outer space.*
Boundary *a line that marks the limit of an area. A border, an edge.*
Peninsula *land surrounded on three sides by water.*
Delmarva *a peninsula named for the three states owning parts of it---Delaware, Maryland and Virginia.*
Survey *a way of finding the exact location and amount of land area. Surveyors use geometry and trigonometry. A survey measures land.*

While Pennsylvania and Maryland were still English colonies and there was as yet no United States, the two colonies argued over boundary lines. Each wanted all the land they could get!

At last, in 1763, two astronomer - mathematicians were given the work of surveying an exact line between the two colonies. From 1763 to 1767 Charles Mason and Jeremiah Dixon worked at finding and marking a line, running east to west, between Pennsylvania and Maryland. At the western end of their line they began to have trouble with Indians and had to stop their survey!

To this day the northern boundary line of our state is called the "Mason-Dixon Line." It is often thought of as the dividing line between the northern and southern states in our nation.

Not many people know that before Mason and Dixon finished that northern boundary of Maryland, they surveyed another line. If you look at your map, Figure 1,

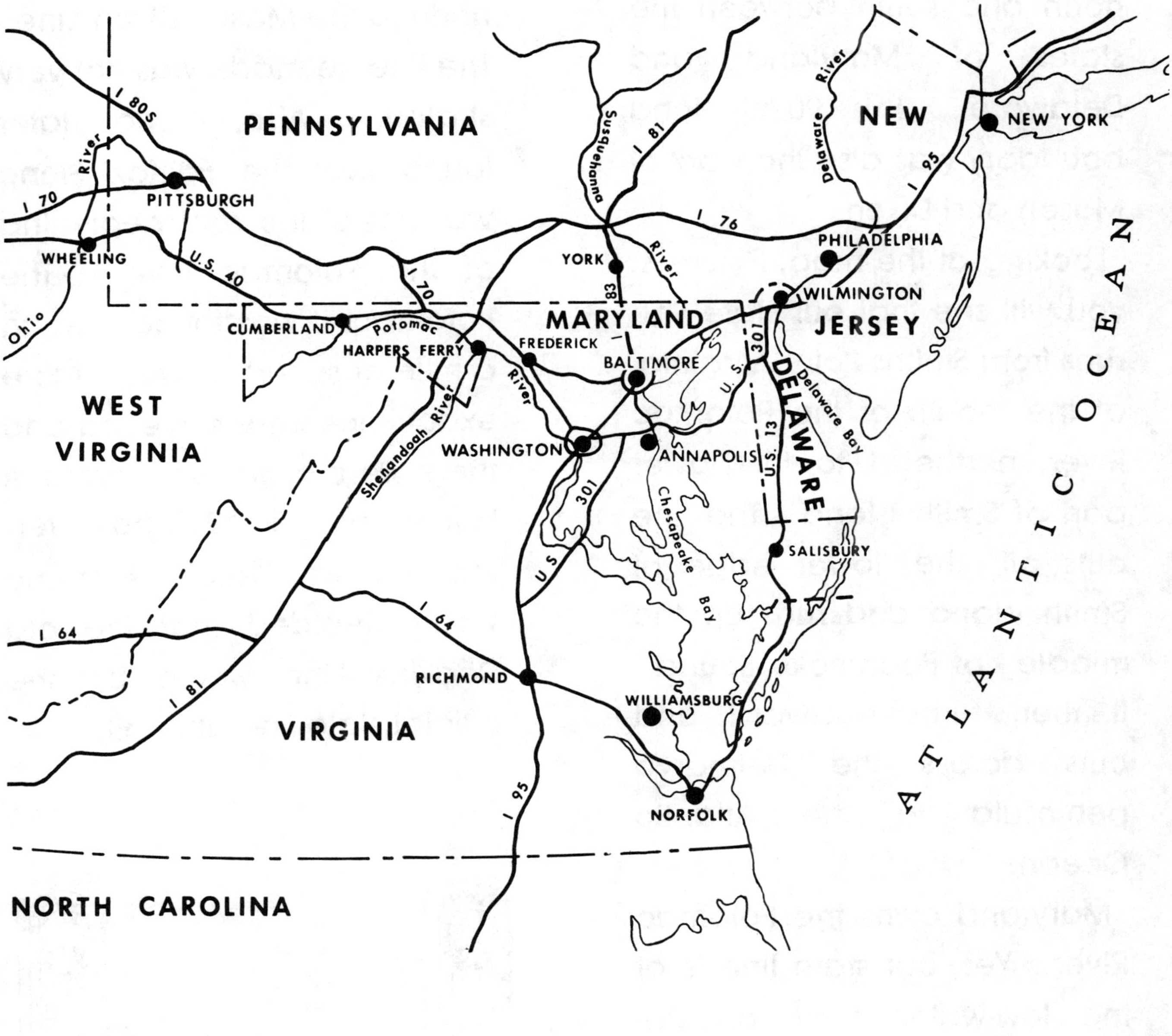

Maryland and surrounding states.

Courtesy Maryland State Dept. of Economic and Community Development, Department of State Planning. From *Maryland Historical Atlas,* 1973.

you will see a line that goes north and south between the states of Maryland and Delaware. This 90-mile-long boundary was also the work of Mason and Dixon.

Looking at the map, Figure 1, you will see that our state line runs from Smiths Point, Virginia, at the mouth of the Potomac River, northeast to the lower part of Smith Island. The line cuts off the lower edge of Smith Island and runs up the middle of Pocomoke Sound. It then turns eastward and cuts across the Delmarva peninsula to the Atlantic Ocean.

Maryland owns the Potomac River. Yes, our state line is at the low-water mark on the Virginia bank of the Potomac!

Maryland's western border was supposed to start where the Potomac River began and to extend northward. This boundary was first measured by a man called Deakins. He ran it from the "Fairfax Stone" north to the Mason-Dixon Line. The line he made was not very straight! Also, it was later found that the Fairfax Stone was not at the real beginning of the Potomac River. The Potomac, it was found, began a mile or so further west. More exact lines were surveyed and there were arguments over the boundary. In 1912, however, the United States Supreme Court decided that the old Deakins Line would be the official state line after all.

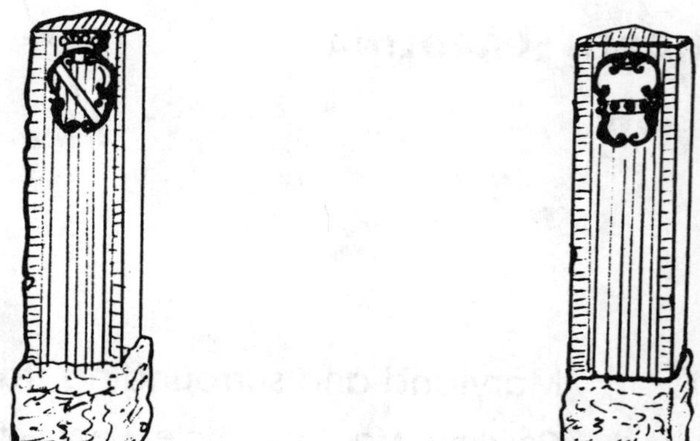

Markers left by Mason and Dixon along the Maryland-Pennsylvania border.

Exercise.

You can learn much from the map in Figure 1. Get out a sheet of paper, please, and write out the answers to the following questions.

REMEMBER ---***The Potomac River begins*** at the south corner of Garrett County and is the southern boundary of Maryland all the way down past St. Mary's County.

(1) Maryland touches four other states. What are their names?

(2) Looking at your map in Figure 1, you can see that eight Maryland counties touch the edge of the state of Pennsylvania. Name these counties.

(3) Three of our counties touch the state of West Virginia. List the names of these counties, please.

(4) Delaware takes up much of the Delmarva peninsula. Name the seven Maryland counties touching the edge of the state of Delaware.

(5) On the ***Eastern Shore*** of Maryland two counties touch edge of the state of Virginia! Name them please.

(6) Working from near the western side of the map, see as you come eastward down the Potomac River (include Washington County), that eight Maryland counties border Virginia. The Potomac River is the boundary between these Maryland counties and the state of Virginia. List these counties please.

(7) NOW! Here is a real "brain-twister"! Which county in Maryland touches the edges of THREE STATES? Name these three states.

(8) What state owns the Potomac River?

(10) We love our Maryland beaches on the Atlantic Ocean. Do the Maryland Atlantic beaches form a part of the eastern boundary of Maryland?

4. MARYLAND'S BIG GIFT TO OUR NATION

Capital	*a capital city, a seat of government.*
Capitol	*a building in which a government meets.*
Federal	*meaning national; a federation of states.*
Fall Line	*a place where streams begin to flow over rocks and waterfalls; boats find it hard to go upstream. Where rising land causes fast water, rapids.*
Parallelogram	*a figure with four sides with opposite sides parallel.*
Rapids	*a place where water moves swiftly over a rocky stream bed.*

More About Square Miles

We have learned that a square mile ***can*** be any shape at all! But remember, one square mile of area will ***always*** contain the same amount of land or water surface.

DISCUSS this please. Draw several examples of shapes that might contain one square mile of surface. Why should this be very easy?

Also, square miles do not always come out even! You may have a part of a mile, a fraction, left over. A surveyor might measure land and find that it has an area of $7\frac{1}{2}$ square miles or $5\frac{1}{4}$ square miles.

If the area you are studying is a square or a parallelogram, it is very easy to find out how many square miles are inside. You measure the height of the figure, then measure its width. Now multiply height by width. DISCUSS this and make up some examples.

When the United States had only thirteen states, President Washington was asked to pick a place to build a fine new "Federal City." They asked him to look along the Potomac

River. The Congress had met and decided that the national capital should be as near the center of the country as possible. (Is Washington, D. C. near the middle of our nation today? No!)

George Washington picked a place just below the "fall line" of the Potomac River. This was the place where rocks and rapids made it impossible for ships to come any farther up the river. Here, he decided, would be the new capital of our new nation. It was far enough from the ocean to be fairly safe from attack from the sea. The Potomac River would be a nice waterway for the city. People could travel on the river. Cargo could be brought to the city by ship.

George Washington asked Virginia and Maryland to give a large square of land to the federal government. This was in the year 1790.

The next year, President Washington asked that boundaries be surveyed and marked. Daniel Carroll and Thomas Johnson of Maryland, and David Stuart of Virginia, were chosen to do this work.

The square of land Washington chose was ten miles long and ten miles wide. How many square miles does this square contain?

Some of it, as you can see by our sketch, is water area. The state of Virginia gave about 36 square miles of land. Maryland gave about 60 square miles of land.

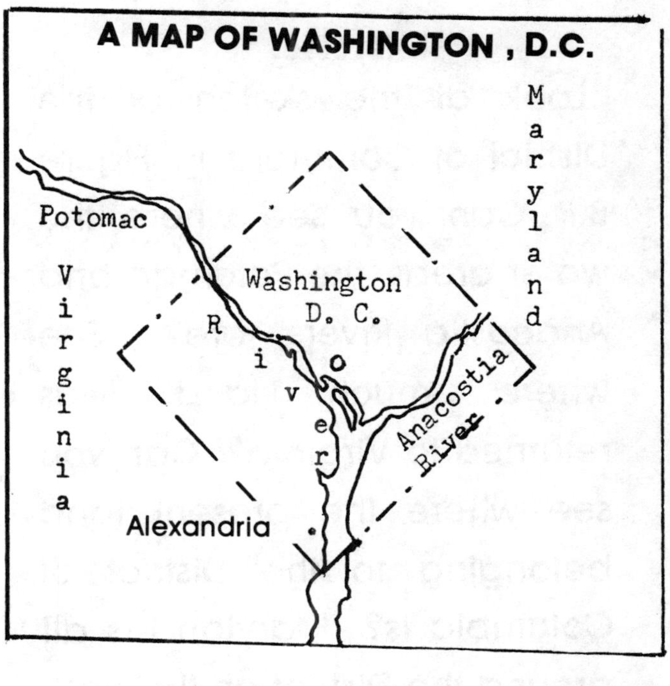

FIGURE B.

The Virginia land included the city of Alexandria. Soon the people of Alexandria felt unhappy with being a part of the capital city. They said that they were not getting much benefit from the United States government. They said that all the government buildings were being put up on the ***other side*** of the river. Also, said the Virginians to the members of Congress, the capital city would probably ***never*** need all this land anyway! So in 1846, Congress gave most of the Virginia land back to Virginia.

Exercise.

Look at the sketch of the District of Columbia in Figure B. Can you see where the water areas, the Potomac and Anacostia Rivers, are? See where much land was returned to Virginia? Can you see where the present land belonging to the District of Columbia is? Maryland is all around the District on the east. Can you see where this is? Virginia land near the District is west of the Potomac River. Can you see this? Learning about directions, such as east and west, will help you read all maps.

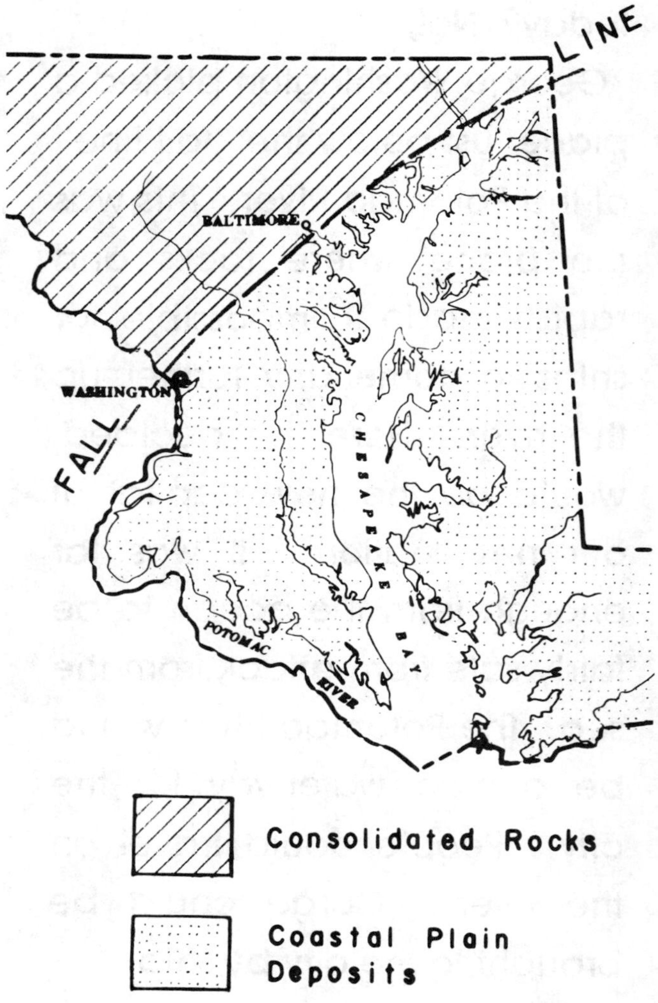

The general type of soil and rock in Maryland. Notice the Fall Line.

Courtesy Maryland Geological Survey.

From *Water in Maryland* Patrick Walker.

SECTION II.
MARYLAND'S PHYSICAL GEOGRAPHY

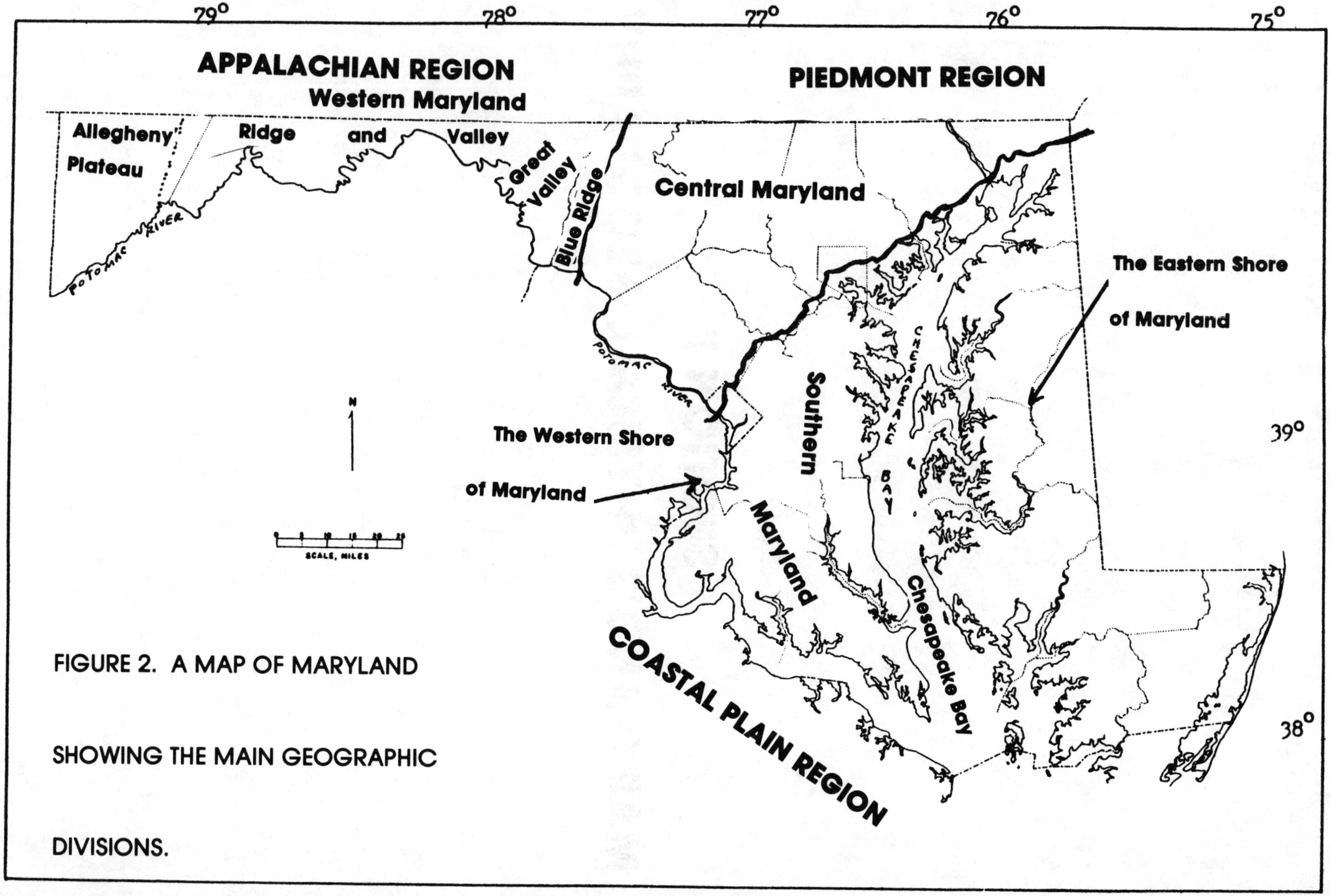

FIGURE 2. A MAP OF MARYLAND

SHOWING THE MAIN GEOGRAPHIC

DIVISIONS.

Impressed *strongly affected by something.*
Navigable *deep enough for ocean-going ships.*
Piedmont *land at the foot of mountains; hilly country.*

Your parents will be impressed when you use these next two words. You may find them a little hard to fit into a conversation!

Geology is said "gee-ol-o-gee." It is the study of the forms, natural processes, and structures of the crust of our earth. IMPORTANT: Look up "geology" in your encyclopedia. List the things that geologists study. Would you like to be a geologist?

Physiography is the science of describing the earth. You say it, "fizz-ee-og-rah-fee." This branch of geology tells us about the natural shape and form of our earth, its ***physical geography,*** the landscape.

Now, muttering these two impressive terms, we are ready to study the geology and physiography of Maryland.

Maryland may be divided, by the way her land is formed, into three parts. You can see the size and location of these by looking at Figure 2. The parts are: the ***Coastal Plain,*** the ***Piedmont,*** and the ***Appalachian*** regions.

1. THE COASTAL PLAIN REGION

About half the land area of our state is in the part called the Coastal Plain. This plain is a part of a much larger one called the ***Atlantic Coastal Plain.***

The Atlantic Coastal Plain extends from Florida to Massachusetts. It is fairly level land which slopes out into the Atlantic Ocean. It slopes out, in fact, from 75 to 100 miles. Then the ocean becomes very deep. That part of the plain lying just offshore under the Atlantic Ocean is know as the "continental shelf."

Our dry land part of this Atlantic Colastal Plain is an area of about 5,000 square miles. The Maryland Coastal Plain is divided into two parts by Chesapeake Bay. (See Figure 2). These parts are called the ***Eastern Shore*** of Maryland and the ***Western Shore*** of Maryland.

The Coastal Plain is not very high above the level of the ocean water (sea level). The Eastern Shore section is very low and flat. Its streams move slowly down to the bays and the ocean. On the Western Shore the land is a little higher and has hills. The streams there flow down steeper slopes, so they move faster and have cut deeper stream beds. All of Maryland's navigable streams are in the Coastal Plain region.

The Cliffs of Calvert (aerial view).

J. H. Cromwell photograph.

Far back in time, our part of the Atlantic coast was higher above the ocean level than it is now. A deep river valley was cut down to the sea. When the land became lower, the ocean flooded this valley and it became our Chesapeake Bay. The Bay is 185 miles long.

On Chesapeake Bay in Calvert County is a world-famous place. It is called the ***Calvert Cliffs.*** Scientists come from all over the world to see the many fossils (remains of plants and animals preserved for great periods of time) which are found in the sands and clays of the cliffs. The Calvert Cliffs rise from 50 to 100 feet above Chesapeake Bay. They stretch along the western shoreline of the Bay for 30 miles.

The rocks of the Coastal Plain are of the loose kind. They are gravels, sands, clays and silts which have settled out of slow-moving water. Conditions have not been right to make these hard rock.

Soils of the Coastal Plain are sandy or silty, and tend to be light in texture. Except for the great swamps and tide-covered marshes of the Eastern Shore, the land is good for farming.

Iron ore is found in the Coastal Plain region on both sides of Chesapeake Bay. It was mined in colonial days.

The Eastern Shore soil is very good for raising vegetables. The land is ***very*** flat. The marshes shelter wildlife. Deer, small animals and many birds live in the marshes. The waterways and the Chesapeake Bay along the Eastern Shore are good places to fish for fun and for profit.

Over on the Western Shore the soil is not so light or sandy. It more often will contain clay. The five counties of the Western Shore are called ***Southern Maryland.*** Good soil and a warm climate make this section a fine place to raise tobacco. Nearly all of the tobacco raised in our state is grown there.

Exercise.

Turn to your map (Figure 2) please. Can you locate the ***Coastal Plain*** part of Maryland? See the Eastern Shore. Point to the Western Shore.

2. THE PIEDMONT REGION

Our Piedmont region is also called ***Central Maryland.*** As You can see from the map in Figure 2, The Piedmont region begins at the "Fall line." This is where the ground has hard rock under it and slopes more. It is higher above sea level than the Coastal Plain.

Because of the steeper slope of the land, streams run faster in the Piedmont than they do in the Coastal Plain. Stream beds are rocky and full of rapids. The Piedmont area ends at Catoctin Mountain.

Again, just as our Coastal Plain is part of a larger plain, our Piedmont region, too, is part of a ***larger*** Piedmont area. The states to the north and south of us also have Piedmont sections. In Maryland, the Piedmont area makes up

Great Falls of the Potomac River.

J. H. Cromwell photograph.

about one-fourth of our land area. It contains around 2,500 square miles. Land here is rolling, higher above sea level than the Coastal Plain and rather hilly.

Rocks and Soil of the Piedmont Region

Beneath the soil of the Piedmont region is a kind of rock called "crystalline." This is a hard, very old rock. Farmers in Piedmont areas are quite apt to find rocks in their fields. Soils tend to be medium in texture (feel). The land, except for some rocky slopes, is good for raising livestock and crops.

Most of the money made in mining Maryland rock is made from sand, gravel and crushed stone. Limestone is used to make lime and cement products.

We also have Maryland quarries that give us beautiful building stone. These are not as busy as they once were. Several are located in the Piedmont region. They can produce marble, granite, gabbro, quartzite, serpentine, and schist. Many interesting metals have been found in the Piedmont area---gold, iron, chromium, copper and others. Few metals have been mined at a profit.

Exercise.

Turn to your map, Figure 2. Locate the "Piedmont Region."

3. THE APPALACHIAN REGION

(In this section you will find several words that ***look alike!*** *Study the following words until you can correctly spell and define them.)*

Allegany County *a county in Western Maryland.*
Allegheny *a section of high country that is a part of the Appalachian chain of mountains. Scientific name is a"dissected plateau."*
Appalachian *a chain of mountains extending from Canada to Georgia.*
Erosion *wearing away of something by something else! Soil and rock are worn away by water, wind, plants growing, chemical action.*
Extends *stretches out to; reaches out to.*
Plateau *a high, mainly level place; a tableland.*

Our Appalachian mountain section is an important and beautiful part of Maryland. This book divides the state into a coastal plain, a piedmont, and a mountain region. So we will talk of this mountain (Appalachian) region as having four parts.

As you can see, Figure 2, these are: ***Blue Ridge, Great Valley, Valley and Ridge,*** and the ***Allegheny Plateau.*** This area is also often called ***Western Maryland.***

The mountain section contains about 2,000 square miles of land.

On your map in Figure 2, you can see that the ***Blue Ridge*** is located at the western edge of the Piedmont section. Ridges of mountains here cross the state in lines that run north and south. The mountains continue far to the north and south of Maryland. Beyond the Blue Ridge, going west, is the ***Great Valley.*** This valley, also, is not just in Maryland but continues both to the north

Swallow Falls, Garrett County, a popular cascade in the Youghiogheny River, Swallow Falls State Park.

J. H. Cromwell photograph.

and the south. It is, in fact, a thousand miles long! Each state has a different name for its part of the Great Valley! We call our section the ***Hagerstown Valley.*** Across its broad, gently rolling floor the Potomac flows from west to east in great curves.

Going westward from the Great Valley you cross ***tall*** mountains and deep valleys. This part of the Appalachian area is called the ***Valley and Ridge*** section. Ridges of steep mountains cross Maryland here, running north and south.

Now, further west in the eastern part of Garrett County , we find the beginning of the Allegheny Plateau. Most of Garrett County is in the Allegheny Plateau. This big, high, tableland is the highest part of our state. There the mountain tops sometimes reach over 3,000 feet above sea level. Though high, the land is more level and the slopes are less steep than in the Valley and Ridge section. Streams have cut deep valleys with very steep sides through the Plateau. Generally, however, the land does not have the sudden up-and-down slope that the Valley and Ridge section has.

The steeper the slope of the ground, the faster water flows downhill. Can you see why this is? Is this why streams in

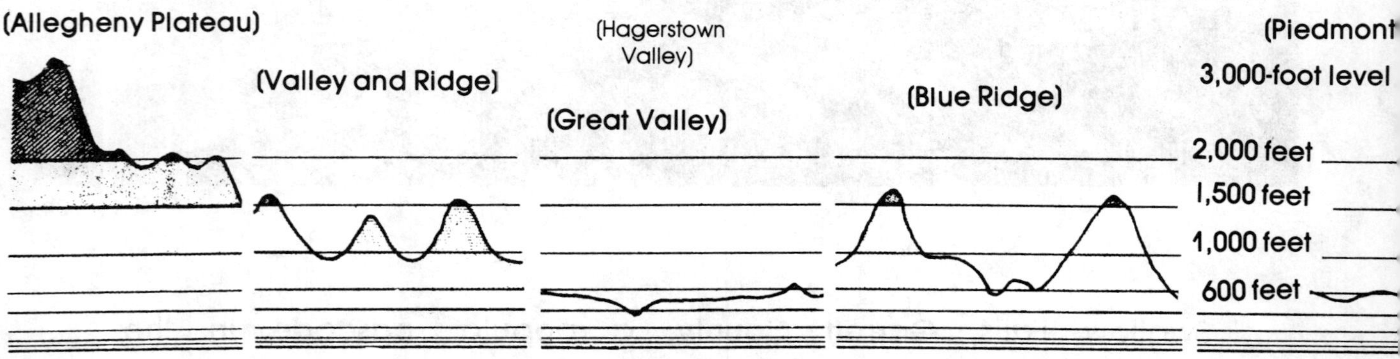

TYPICAL ELEVATIONS IN MARYLAND'S MOUNTAIN (APPALACHIAN) AREA

An old barn in Garrett County near Deep Creek Lake.

J. H. Cromwell photograph.

mountain sections of Maryland rush very fast toward the sea? This also causes them to dig deep stream beds. Where mountain streams flow over the edges of cliffs, they make beautiful waterfalls. Mountain streams are often full of rapids.

Rocks and Soil of the Appalachian Region.

As you might expect in the middle of such a steep land, much of the soil has washed away. This has left rock exposed. Mountains here were formed by the erosion of soil and softer rock. This left ridges of stronger rock behind.

Erosion is caused by water, wind, the action of plants, chemical action, and the movement of sands. DISCUSS this please.

Under the mountain surface are layers of rock which have been folded in ages past. As you might guess, it takes great force and a long time for rock layers to fold.

Some kinds of rock found in the Appalachian region tell scientists that some volcanic action took place here, mostly in the Blue Ridge. DISCUSS ***volcanic*** action. What is it?

Soil in the valleys and on the lower mountain slopes is usually medium to heavy in texture. It is well drained! The soils are quite rich and easily farmed, except on the steeper slopes. There are some parts of the Appalachian area in which the soil is just a shallow

A ski lodge at the WISP ski area, Deep Creek Lake, Garrett County near Oakland, Maryland. J. H. Cromwell photograph.

layer with rock right beneath it. Here, crops suffer in dry years. Orchards, stock farms and crop farms cover the lower mountain slopes and the rich valleys.

Since the mountain sides are too steep and rocky to be farmed, this land is kept for timber. Forests are very valuable for several reasons. Trees grow in forests. These can be cut for lumber and posts.

The forests shelter wildlife and give us places to hunt, hike and fish.

A very valuable thing about woods, too, is that they help prevent erosion, help conserve water and help prevent floods.

The roots of the trees help hold the soil in place. Water which falls into woods (rain and snow) is slowed down by branches and leaves and is given a chance to sink into the soil. Rain falling into a forest does not strike bare ground and rush off, carrying soil with it. Instead rain drops from leaf to leaf and onto moss and leaves below.

Water which runs off bare

land can soon silt up waterways. Then too, water reaching rivers too fast can make them overflow and flood land near the river.

Exercise.

Can you see the Appalachian Mountain Region on the map (Figure 2)?

Maryland snow scene.

J. H. Cromwell photograph.

Muddy Creek Falls, created by Muddy Creek flowing from the Cranesville Swamp.

J. H. Cromwell photograph.

Baltimore County Court House, Towson, Maryland.

J. H. Cromwell photograph.

SECTION III. OUR COUNTIES

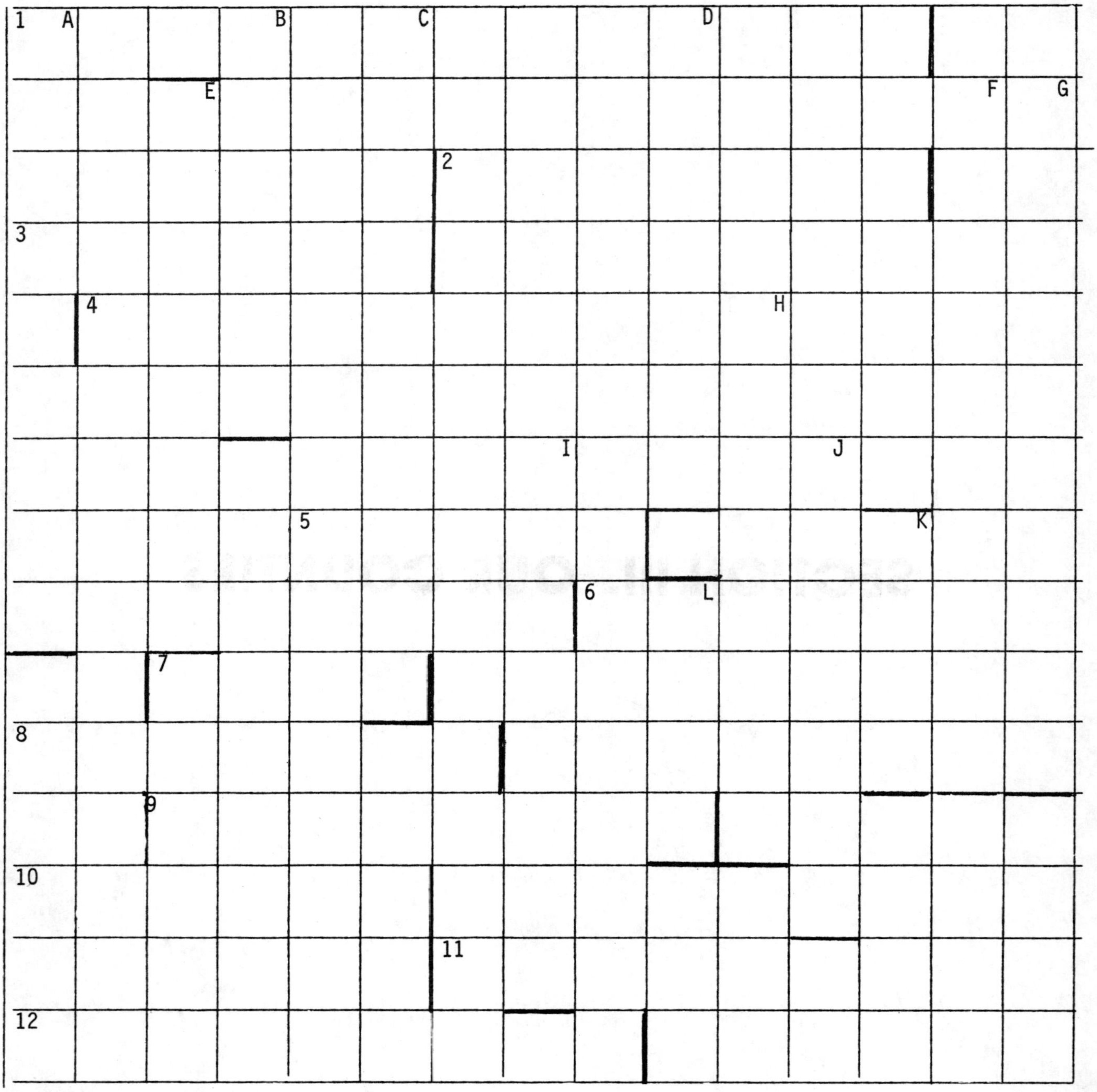
1 A B C D
E F G
2
3
4 H
I J
5 K
6 L
7
8
9
10
11
12

1. A "COUNTY-COUNTING" WORD PUZZLE

★★

County *the largest division for local government in most states.*
County seat *town or city where county government is located. The county capital.*

Your teacher may make copies of this crossword puzzle for you, or you may use a piece of paper for your answers.

When you have finished working this word puzzle, you will know the names of all 23 counties and Baltimore City. This will help you to locate them, too. Use the map (Figure 3) to help you solve the puzzle.

ACROSS WORDS

1. I have one of the world's busiest ocean ports. I am not a county! (13 letters are in my name).
2. I'm between the Potomac and Patuxent rivers. La Plata is my county seat. (7 letters).
3. Easton is my county seat. I'm on the Eastern Shore. (6 letters).
4. I'm growing fast and am nicknamed "P. G." I'm named for a Prince whose name was ----6 letters long.
5. I am Maryland's most north-eastern county. (5 letters).
6. No Maryland county is further west! (7 letters).
7. Name the Saint for whom this county was named. (4 letters).

8. I'm named for the family which first settled Maryland. I'm between Chesapeake Bay and the Patuxent River. (7 letters).

9. My county seat is Denton. Caroline Kennedy and I have something in common. I'm an Eastern Shore county. (8 letters).

10. Ellicott City is my county seat. The Patapsco River is part of my northern boundary. (6 letters).

11. I am the only Maryland county with an Atlantic Ocean beach! (9 letters).

12. My county seat is Frederick. I'm a Piedmont county. I'm named for the Sixth Lord Baltimore, some people say. (9 letters).

DOWN WORDS

(A) I hold Baltimore City in my arms. My marble is famous. (9 letters).

(B) I am an Eastern Shore county beside Chesapeake Bay. The Choptank River is my eastern boundary line. (6 letters).

(C) The Potomac River is my county line on the southwest. Rockville is the capital of this county. (10 letters).

(D) I am named for one of the signers of the Declaration of Independence. My county seat is Westminster. Pennsylvania is north of me. (7 letters).

(E) I am in the Maryland Valley and Ridge section. West Virginia is south of me and Pennsylvania is to the north. (8 letters).

(F) I have water on three sides of me. Look for me between the Choptank and Nanticoke rivers. (10 letters).

(G) My county seat is in Maryland's Great Valley area (Hagerstown Valley). My boundaries touch three states! I'm named for a man who was brave and honest and who did a great deal for our nation. (10 letters).

(H) I touch the state of Virginia. My county seat is Princess Anne. (8 letters).

(I) The Pocomoke River is my eastern boundary. Salisbury is my county seat. The Nanticoke River is my western county line. (8 letters).

(J) I'm named for the last English proprietor (owner) of Maryland. The Susquehanna River is my northeastern boundary. (7 letters).

(K) The Sassafras River is my northern boundary. I'm ***close*** to Delaware! (4 letters).

(L) Two counties and a town are named for this English Queen. Her name is four letters long.

A Schweizer sailplane. Sailplanes often fly from the airport at Frederick, Maryland. These soaring aircraft are towed aloft by light planes, then set free to ride the air---without engines.

Photograph courtesy the Schweizer Aircraft Corp.

Fox hunting in Baltimore County is a colorful activity.

J. H. Cromwell photograph.

2. YOUR COUNTY (A LOOK INTO A CRYSTAL BALL!)

Would you like to find out something that very few people know about ***your county?*** By working the problem below, putting the numbers on a piece of paper, you can find out how many people are living in your county NOW.

Every ten years a national census (count) is taken. One was taken in 1970. The last one was taken in 1980.

Use the Table in Section IX, which gives county population facts. On a separate piece of paper:

(a) Put the 1980 population count.

(b) Below this put the 1970 population census count.

(c) Now subtract the smaller number from the larger one to get the answer.

(If your county is growing in population the top number (a) will be bigger. If this is so, your answer will be a plus (+) number. If your county is losing people the bottom number (b) will be larger. Then your answer will be a minus (−) number. Put a plus or a minus by your answer, please.)

Take the answer you found by subtracting and divide it by 10. Write down the number you found when you divided. This number is the ***average*** number of people gained, or lost, each year by your county.

Yes, this same system will work to find the population trends for Baltimore City.

How can you find out how many people will probably be living in your county five years from 1980?

You can take the number of

people gained or lost each year and multiply this number by 5. Add or subtract this number to the 1980 census count and you'll have the number of people for 1985.

True, this ***is*** just a guess. It is also called an estimate or a ***projection.*** But this is an estimate built upon facts.

What might change your projection? More jobs? Fewer jobs? DISCUSS other things that might make a city or county gain or lose residents.

Also DISCUSS, THE QUESTION "Is growth ***always*** a good thing?"

3. COUNTY CAPITALS

Activity

DRAW AN OUTLINE OF YOUR COUNTY. In large letters put the name of the county on your outline. Place the county seat with a small circle. Write the name of the county seat beside the circle. Put the latest estimate of the number of people (population) in your county on your outline map in black numbers. Color your map a pale color.

The capital of your county is where the county government is located. This is called a "county seat."

Your teacher will tell you whether or not to use the map in Figure 3 to help you as you work out the following word problem.

READY? MATCH each county to its county seat by writing A through X down one side of your paper. Then put the right number for that county's capital, county seat, beside the letters.

If Maryland has 23 counties, why have we 24 names in the list? Yes, it is because Maryland has 23 counties ***and*** Baltimore City.

County

(A) Baltimore City
(B) Allegany
(C) Anne Arundel
(D) Baltimore County
(E) Calvert
(F) Caroline
(G) Carroll
(H) Cecil
(I) Charles
(J) Dorchester
(K) Frederick
(L) Garrett
(M) Harford
(N) Kent
(O) Howard
(P) Montgomery
(Q) Prince George's
(R) Queen Anne's
(S) St. Mary's
(T) Somerset
(U) Talbot
(V) Washington
(W) Wicomico
(X) Worcester

County Seat

(1) Snow Hill
(2) Frederick
(3) Leonardtown
(4) Princess Anne
(5) Easton
(6) Hagerstown
(7) Baltimore City
(8) Salisbury
(9) Centreville
(10) Upper Marlboro
(11) Rockville
(12) Chestertown
(13) Bel Air
(14) Oakland
(15) Cumberland
(16) Annapolis
(17) Towson
(18) Prince Frederick
(19) Elkton
(20) La Plata
(21) Cambridge
(22) Westminster
(23) Denton
(24) Ellicott City

Carroll County Court House, Westminster, Md.

J. H. Cromwell photograph.

4. MAP WORK

Use a map like the one shown below and DRAW a line out from the center of each county to a clear space. At the end of the line put the name of that county's capital, its county seat. Do this for all 23 counties, but not for Baltimore City. PLAN your lines so that they won't criss-cross and so that you will have room to write out your information!

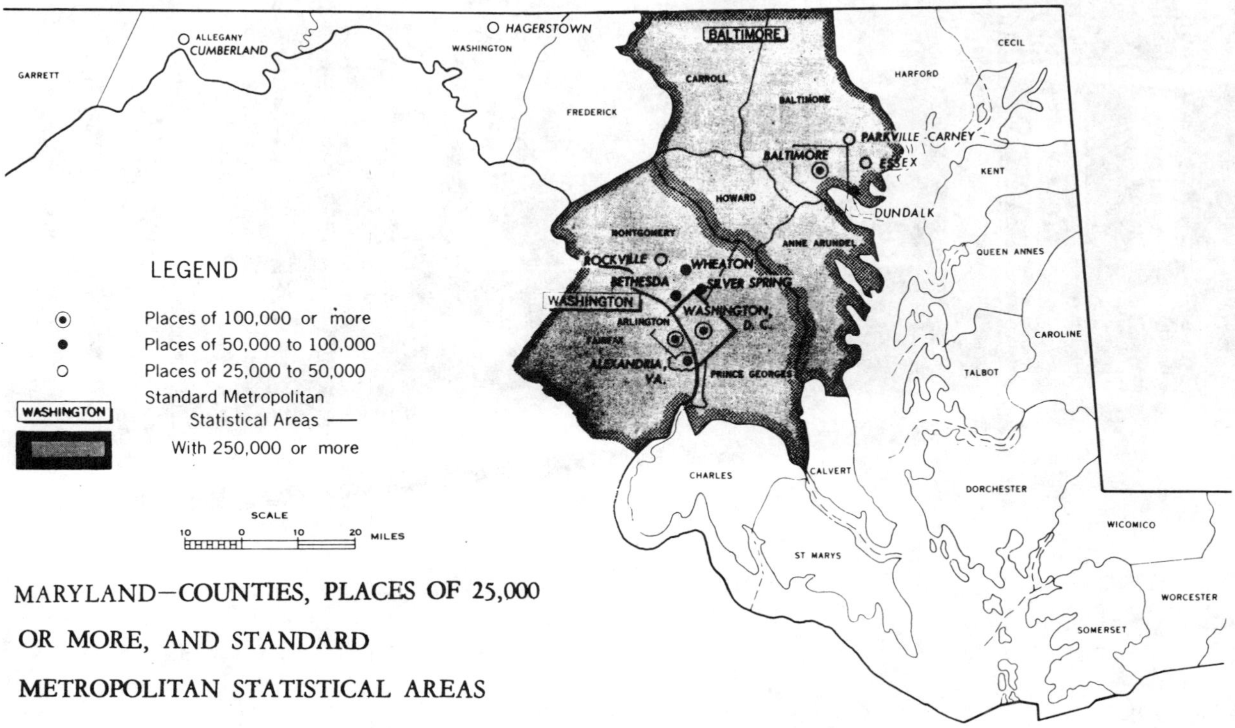

MARYLAND—COUNTIES, PLACES OF 25,000 OR MORE, AND STANDARD METROPOLITAN STATISTICAL AREAS

U.S. DEPARTMENT OF COMMERCE
BUREAU OF THE CENSUS

Barbara Fritchie House and Museum, Frederick, Maryland.

J. H. Cromwell photograph.

SECTION IV. MARYLAND WEATHER

Clouds float lazily over this Maryland farm in Cecil County.

J. H. Cromwell photograph.

Average Annual Temperature *average temperature for the year.*
Climate *average condition of the weather of a certain place; a summary of day-to-day weather conditions.*
Elevation *the height of a land surface above sea level.*
Hurricane *a large storm with high winds, rain, thunder and lightning.*
Latitude *the distance north or south of the equator of a place.*
Tornado *very dangerous, whirling storm with a narrow path, very high winds.*

If you average out all the things that make the weather of a place for several years, you can say that these make up its "climate." You would include its heat, cold, humidity (how moist the air is), rainfall, snow, winds and fog. After studying the daily weather of a place for a long time you might decide that it had a mild climate, a dry climate, a hot or a cold climate.

Maryland has a mild climate. Our rainfall is usually quite plentiful. Our coldest month is almost always January and our warmest month is usually July.

Our winds come from the west and the northwest a great deal of the time. We seldom have winds that blow hard enough to hurt our houses or street signs. We do have thunderstorms and a few tornadoes each year. About one hurricane a year passes near enough to Maryland to cause high tides and strong winds, followed by heavy rains. Coastal areas of Maryland are most often brushed by hurricanes. Few of these huge storms get as far inland as the mountains.

Rainfall is measured in inches. Suppose you were standing on a perfectly flat roof. Suppose, too, that water had no way of getting off this roof. If it rains and the water on the roof is an inch deep, then you have had an inch of precipitation. Of course, water falling on the ground

A Maryland snow scene. J. H. Cromwell photograph.

sinks in or runs off, doesn't it? ***Precipitation*** is a word that means water reaching the earth from the air. It includes rain, mist, drizzle, and even snow and hail. We measure the amount of precipitation of snow and hail alone and also say it in terms of how much water the snow or hail would make if melted.

Different parts of Maryland have very different average annual rainfalls. Some parts of the state have as much as 48 inches; others have as little as 35 inches of rain a year.

Our weather is affected by the movement of great air masses. Sometimes cold air pours down from central Canada. It often brings bright, clear, cool weather.

Sometimes warm air swirls up from the Gulf of Mexico, or from the states south of us, and causes cloudy, humid, warm weather.

Several things cause the weather in different parts of the state to be quite varied. The ***elevation*** of the land, the ***latitude*** of a place, the mountains or the presence of

Chesapeake Bay and the ***AtlanticOcean,***large bodies of water,all affect local weather.

As you know, the weather in Garrett County is ***quite*** different from that of Wicomico County. DISCUSS this. It is interesting to understand the weather of the place you live.

TABLE
TEMPERATURES IN MARYLAND

(REGION)	*(ANNUAL AVERAGE TEMPERATURE)*
Western Maryland	*48°F to 52°F*
Piedmont	*52°F to 55°F*
Coastal Plain	*55°F to 58°F*

Elevation

If you get into an airplane and fly it higher and higher, you will find that the air gets cooler. In fact, for each thousand feet you climb, the temperature gets about 3½°F cooler.

If you leave the Coastal Plain part of our state and travel to Western Maryland to the top of a mountain 3,000 feet above sea level, how much would you expect the temperature to drop? This explains several things. It gives us the reason people go to the mountains in the summertime to cool off! It tells us why the growing season is shorter in the mountains. It explains why, sometimes rain will be falling near Baltimore, while in Garrett County snow is falling! DISCUSS this, please.

You can see from the table that the higher the land is, above sea level, the cooler it is.

Latitude

The nearer you are to the equator, the warmer the weather (if your elevation does not change and affect the temperature). In Maryland our most southern counties are a little warmer for this reason---they are further south.

Water Near Land

Water does not change temperature as fast as land does. So, large amounts of water near land will affect the temperature of that land. Chesapeake Bay causes the land near it to be a little warmer in the winter than land located away from the Bay. The Atlantic Ocean, too, affects the temperature along the coast. Also, the ocean near us is warmed by a huge current called the Gulf Stream.

Can you see that in the winter, land near large amounts of water will be warmer, and in the summer it will be a little cooler, than land further from water? The nearness of the water and the air blowing from the land and water areas affect temperature.

Growing Seasons

The usual amount of time from the last frost in spring to the first frost in the fall, is called the "growing season." In Maryland, because of the things we have just learned (about elevation, latitude, water-near-land) the growing season varies. It changes from 225 days at Ocean City to 130 days at Oakland. Most of the state has quite a long growing season.

Exercise. **"BROKEN ENGLISH!"**

Good grief! These sentences below have broken in half! Can you put them back together, please? On a sheet of paper place the letters A through J on the left. On the right side of your paper place the numbers (1) through (10).

Now, DRAW A LINE from the ***letter*** beside the first half of the sentence, over to the ***correct number*** beside the last half. Use a ruler. This is not an easy task, so work slowly to get a sentence completed.

(A) The kind of weather an area has is called	*(1) average annual temperature of about 48°F to 52°F.*
(B) The higher you go	*(2) the Gulf of Mexico and sometimes the states south of us.*
(C) Western counties have an	*(3) average annual temperature of about 52°F to 55°F.*
(D) The further toward the equator you go	*(4) its temperature as fast as land does.*
(E) The Piedmont section has an	*(5) January will be our coldest month.*
(F) You can be sure that	*(6) the colder you get.*
(G) The Coastal Plain section has an	*(7) its climate.*
(H) Water does not change	*(8) the warmer you get (at sea level).*
(I) Warm, moist air swirls into Maryland from	*(9) average annual temperature of about 55°F to 58°F.*
(J) Our winds are most often	*(10) from the west and northwest.*

An old Conestoga-style wagon rests in the snow. Note the fence made from split logs.

J. H. Cromwell photograph.

SECTION V. WATER WEALTH

Can you figure out how this long pole helped bring a bucket up from this old well?

J. H. Cromwell photograph.

Evaporate	*to change from liquid to gas. (Water left in a pan evaporates.)*
Pulley	*rope or cable running over a hanging wheel. Used to lift weights.*
Precipitation	*all forms of falling water (rain, snow, hail, sleet, mist).*
Reservoir	*a place where water is stored; a stream dammed to form a lake.*
Surface	*top layer.*
Water-bearing	*something that carries water; water-carrying.*
Water table	*upper limit of ground completely soaked with water.*

Maryland is rich in water. Though we have dry seasons we usually have plenty of water for our people and our work. We cometimes have trouble building enough reservoirs, pipe lines and water mains (big pipes) to get this water to the people. New homes and businesses in our state keep our water workers very busy!

Each year about 42 inches of rain falls on Maryland. This is an average number. It does not really mean much, because rainfall varies so much around the state. Precipitation varies from 48 inches a year in some places to 35 inches in others.

We have fresh water in streams, springs and wells. We have salt water in much of Chesapeake Bay and in waterways near the Atlantic Ocean. All of our navigable streams are in the Coastal Plain. Many rivers in Maryland are deep enough for boating, however, in other sections. We have no natural lakes.

Our communities get their water in several ways. Some use springs; some use wells. Many take water directly from nearby streams. If necessary, a community will build a dam across a stream so that water can be stored in the lake (reservoir) behind the dam. All of this water must be tested every

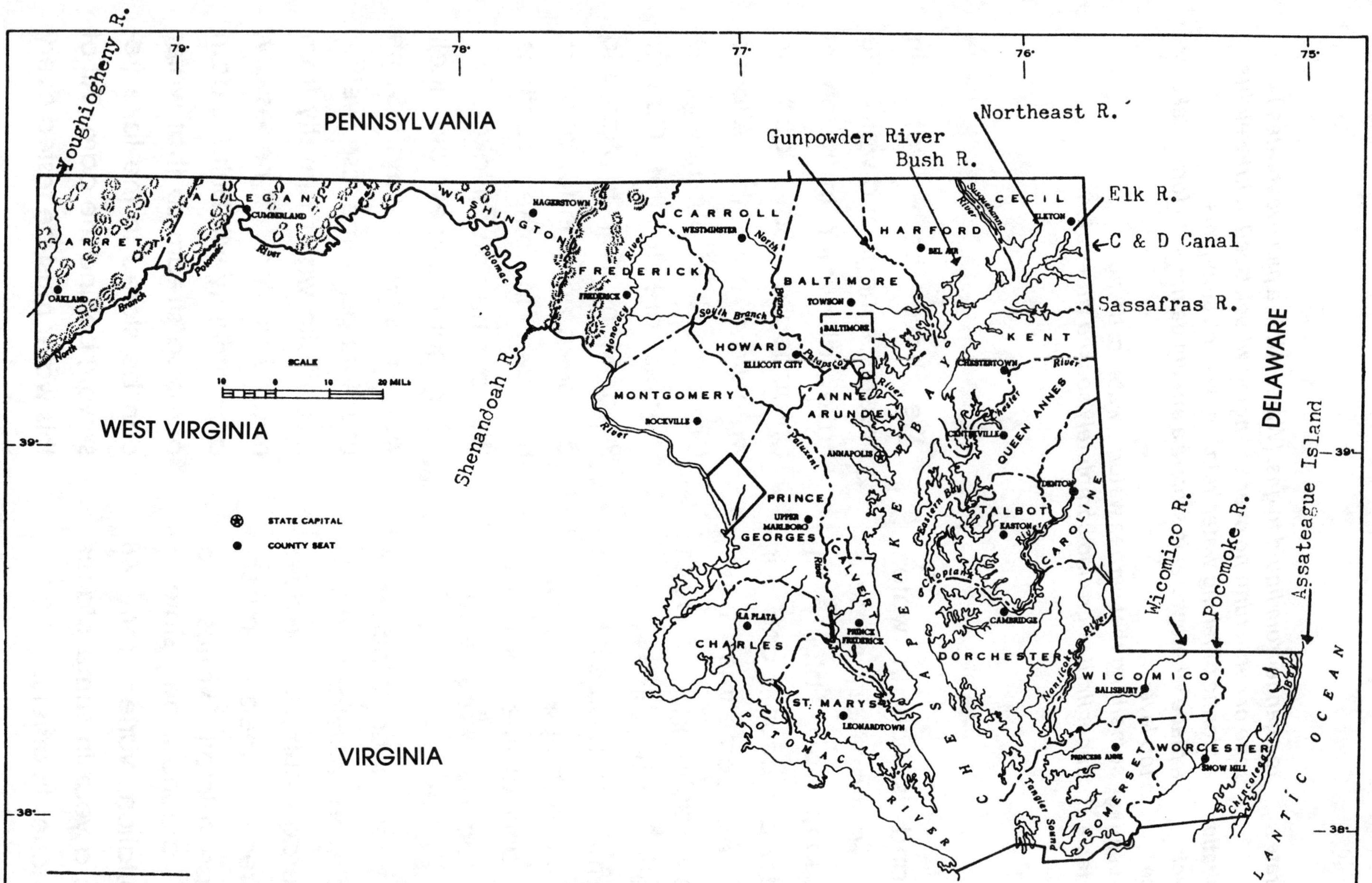

Figure 3. MARYLAND COUNTIES, COUNTY SEATS, MOUNTAINS AND RIVERS.

Map courtesy Bureau of the Census, U.S. Dept. of Commerce.

once in a while to be sure it is safe to drink. Most water used in our towns and cities is treated before use. That is, chlorine and fluorine may be added.

There are laws which help us keep our streams clean. Mines and factories must not let harmful wastes drain into streams. Sewage must be treated before it is allowed to get into streams. We need clean streams for our drinking water, for swimming, and for fishing, too. Water experts advise home builders about septic tanks and wells.

Do you know that water is about 11% hydrogen and 89% oxygen? Water will purify itself by oozing through sands, porous rocks and silt. Towns, however, usually treat water used for homes, just to be sure it is safe to drink.

Conservation of water is important. Forests, wood lots, parks, long strips of trees, shrubs and grass along dual-lane highways, all help us to conserve water! Yes, green things do use water, but they save it by keeping rain from hitting the earth directly. Rain drips down through leaves to the ground. Then, when it gets to the ground there are roots and old leaves to slow it down even more. To slow rain down and give it time to sink into the ground, farmers plant crops in rows that run ***across*** the slope of their land. Does this also help prevent erosion? Yes, bare land is bad because water rushes off it, carrying earth away.

1. SPRINGS AND WELLS

Springs are natural flows of water from the ground. A spring is the overflow of water from a "ground-water reservoir." Ground water is water that has fallen onto the surface and has sunk into the ground.

Springs come up through cracks in rock, or bubble up through the earth. Many towns pipe water from mountain springs located above the town. This saves the cost of pumps because the water flows downhill, pulled by the force of gravity. Springs, of course, should be tested to be sure the water is clean, before being used for drinking water.

Wells are holes in the ground! They can be drilled, of course, for oil or natural gas and other things, but the ones we want to talk about right now, are used for water. There are two kinds of water wells: (1) water-table wells, and (2) artesian wells. The word ***artesian*** is said "are-tease-yun."

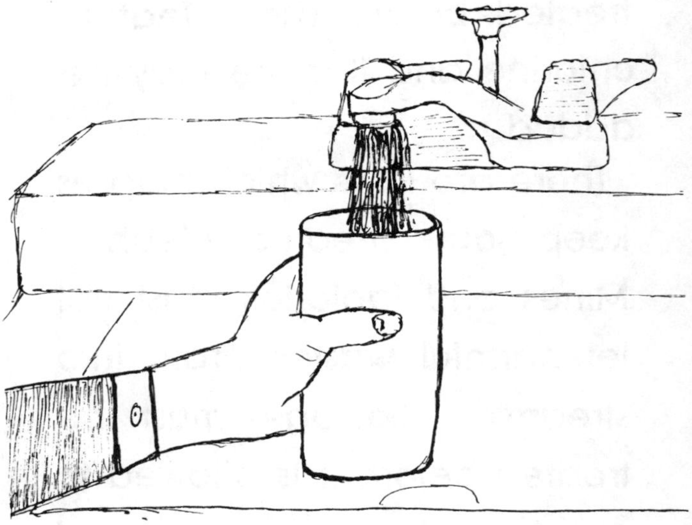

Dinah Fiot drawing.

Water-table wells are dug down into the ground to a level at which water begins to seep in. This level is called the "water-table." It is the top of a layer of water-soaked ground. To get a good flow of water, wells may be dug several feet down into this water-soaked earth.

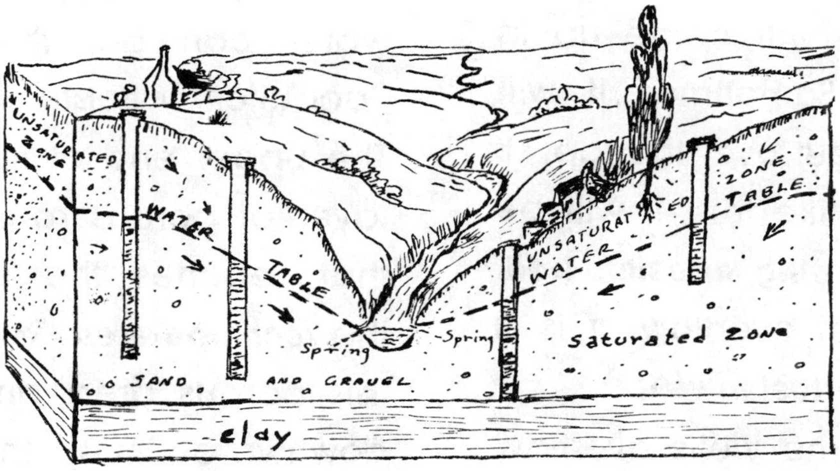

FIGURE C. How the water table follows land surfaces.
(*Courtesy Maryland Geological Survey*).

The ***water table,*** as you can see in this sketch, follows the shape of the land above it. It is, however, nearer the surface in valleys and low places than it is on hills.

Precipitation "feeds" the water table. The water table is refilled most in the time from late fall to early spring. During the summer, people and plants use a lot of water. A great deal is lost due to evaporation. This causes the water table to lower.

If your water-table well goes dry, you can wait for a rain, or you can dig deeper. By digging deeper, you again reach the water table. To get water up out of a well, you must use a pump or a bucket! Some farm homes and vacation homes still have wells which have a rope and a pulley. This is one way to pull buckets of water up out of the well.

Artesian wells are not likely to run dry. The artesian well gets its water from a layer of water-bearing sand or porous rock. This layer, through which water can seep, is trapped below hard rock or heavy clay. (See Figure 4.) When a well is bored down through the rock or clay to the water-bearing layer, water will come up in the well. Sometimes it will come right out over the top. If it overflows like this, it will be called a ***flowing artesian well.*** If it does not overflow, it is a ***non-flowing artesian well.***

Why do some wells overflow and others do not? It depends partly on the elevation of the place where the water first entered the ground, doesn't it? (See Figure 4.) Also, how easily water can get through the "acquifer" affects well flow. The upper end of the slanted layer of porous rock or sand that reaches the surface is the ***recharge area.*** Rain falls on this porous area and trickles downward into the water-bearing layer of sand or porous rock. Water always obeys the pull of gravity. Artesian water moves slowly, three feet a day or less.

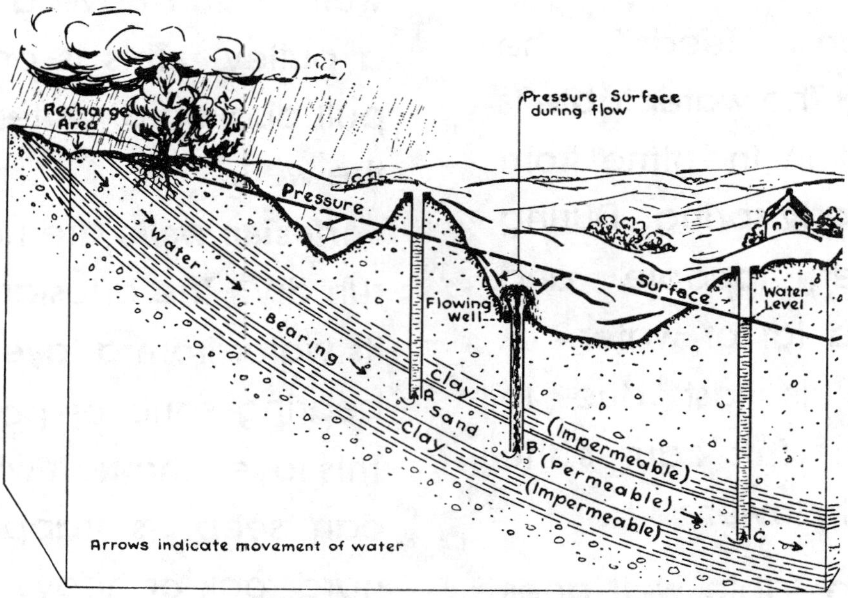

Sketch showing the Principle of Artesian Water Flow

Figure 4. Sketch of Artesian Water Flow.

(Courtesy Maryland Geological Survey)

The following sentences are ones that you would not have understood before our study of Maryland's water!

Most ***ground water*** in our Western and Piedmont counties is found under ***water-table*** conditions. In the Coastal Plain sections, both ***water-table wells*** and ***artesian wells*** are common.

Exercise.

We have been pouring facts into our minds while studying water. We have learned a lot! To be sure of the meaning of important water words, let's review them . WRITE the meanings of the following words on a piece of paper.

Springs are..............................

Reservoirs are ....

The ***water table*** is ....

A ***water-table well*** is ....

Ground water is ....

An ***artesian well*** is ....

PROJECT

Choose one of the following subjects. Look for information in other books. Use a page to draw a picture or diagram. This will show how your subject looks or how it works. Now describe your subject by writing a short report.

Water subjects

(1) Springs
(2) Water-table wells
(3) Reservoirs
(4) Testing water for purity before use

(5) Stopping water pollution
(6) The water table
(7) Artesian wells

2. WHERE DOES WATER GO?

Water flows downhill, pulled by the force of gravity. It keeps moving until it reaches sea level. Tons of water evaporate on the way. Tons are used by plants, people, livestock and wildlife. The water remaining is stubborn! It keeps moving on down toward the ocean.

Where does our Maryland water go? Most of our precipitation drains off into the Potomac River and Chesapeake Bay. We call the Bay and River ***drainage basins.*** This means that these big waterways collect water running off land near them and drain it away. The

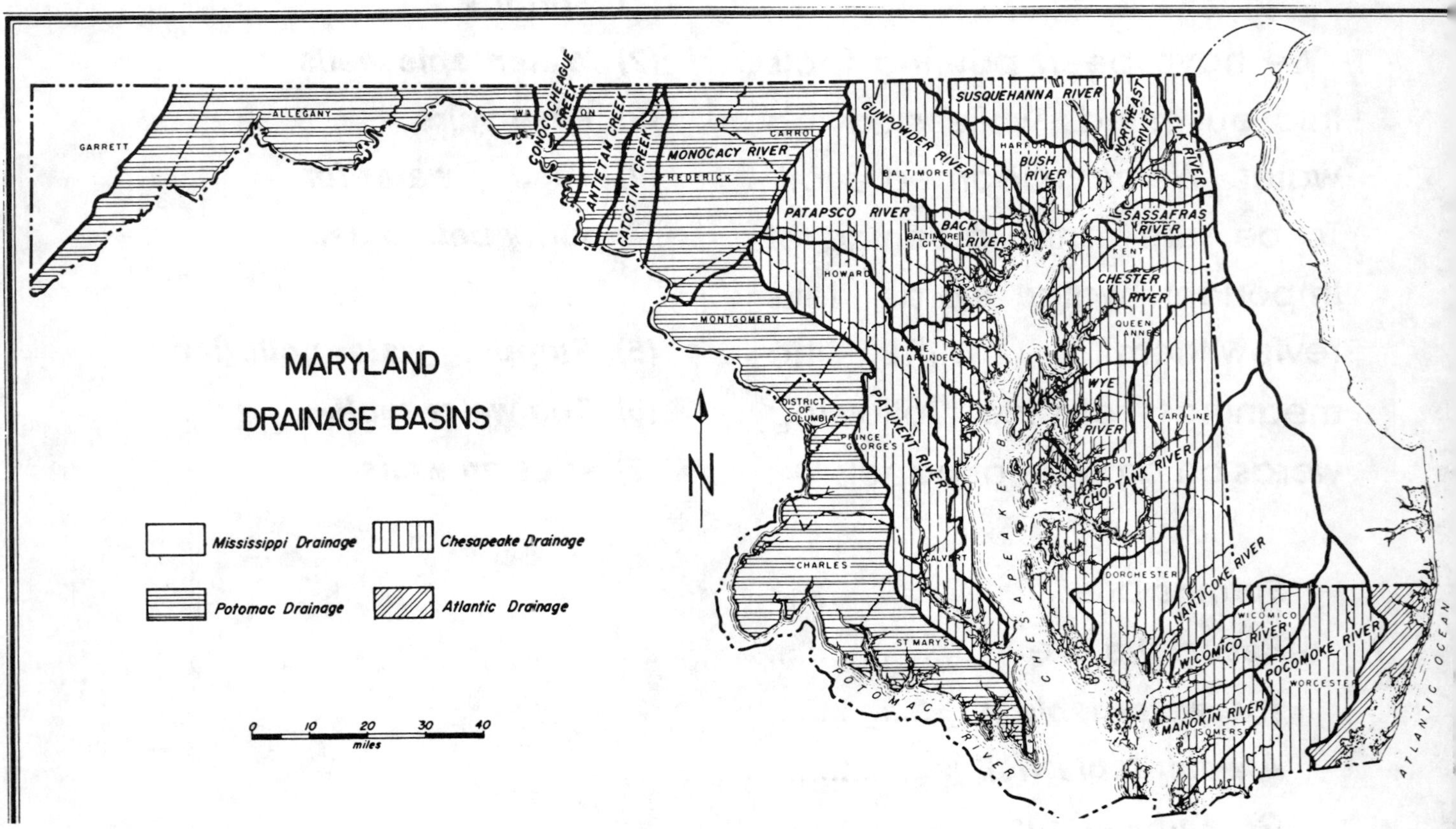

Figure 5. Maryland drainage basins. (Courtesy Maryland Geological Survey).

Potomac flows into Chesapeake Bay. Water from the Bay then goes into the Atlantic Ocean.

Figure 5 shows the five Maryland drainage basins.

The five are:

The ***Youghiogheny River*** which drains most of Garrett County. This Maryland water travels, by way of the Ohio and Mississippi rivers, to the Gulf of Mexico.

The ***Potomac River*** drains eastern Garrett County; all of Allegany, Washington, and Frederick counties; parts of Carroll, Montgomery, Prince George's, Charles and St. Mary's counties.

Western Chesapeake Bay drains Harford, Baltimore, Anne Arundel, Calvert and Howard counties; parts of Cecil, Carroll, Montgomery, Prince George's, Charles and St. Mary's counties.

Eastern Chesapeake Bay drains Kent, Queen Anne's, Talbot, Caroline, Dorchester, Wicomico and Somerset counties; parts of Cecil and Worcester counties.

The ***Atlantic Ocean*** drains (directly), a small part of Worcester county.

Dinah Fiot drawing.

3. OUR STREAMS AND BAYS

Since waterways give us so much pleasure and profit in Maryland, suppose we locate them. Let's ***take a trip*** around the map shown in Figure 3.

We begin our trip at the south corner of Garrett County where the ***Potomac River*** starts its journey to the ocean. Find this point, please. Now, move your finger down the Potomac as it winds down to Washington, D.C. From Washington, see how the Potomac flows on down to Chesapeake Bay.

Going back to Garrett County, locate the ***Youghiogheny River.*** It drains water northward! Most of our Maryland rivers flow easterly or southerly. Locate another beautiful Western Maryland river, the ***Savage River,*** in Garrett County.

The ***Patuxent River*** begins, and is part of, the boundary line between Montgomery and Howard counties. Find this river. See how far the Patuxent goes? It winds all the way down through the Western Shore of Maryland. Where does it end?

(Md. Dept. of Economic Development)

Annapolis Waterfront Today.

In the Annapolis area (locate Annapolis), the ***Severn River,*** the ***South River*** and the ***Magothy River*** have water deep enough for boating.

Ocean-going ships can use the wide, deep channel that wends up Chesapeake Bay. The channel is marked on water charts. It goes all the way to the Port of Baltimore. The Bay is 185 miles long.

The mighty ***Susquehanna River*** enters Chesapeake Bay near the northern end of the Bay. Just south and a little west of the Susquehanna River, is the much smaller ***Gunpowder River.***

Looking again at the northern end of Chesapeake Bay, you can see that the ***Elk River*** leads into the ***Chesapeake and Delaware Canal.*** Big ships can cross from Chesapeake Bay to the Delaware River by using this canal. This saves them a day of travel if they want to go north from the Port of Baltimore.

In colonial days, people would travel as far as they could up the Elk River. Then they would take a stagecoach, ride a horse, or walk over to the Delaware River. There they would get aboard another ship.

The Eastern Shore of Maryland has many rivers! There are so many interesting ones that we do not have space to list them all here. You may want to get a large map of Maryland and study them. We will tell you about several Eastern Shore rivers.

Find the ***Sassafras River,*** please. It is the boundary between Cecil and Kent counties. Farther south you'll see that the ***Chester River*** is a big waterway. The Chester divides Kent County from Queen Anne's County. The ***Miles River*** is used by both work and pleasure boats. The Miles River enters ***Eastern Bay*** on the eastern side of Kent Island. (Locate Eastern Bay.)

The ***Tred Avon River*** is a waterway leading to the city of Easton in Talbot County.

The ***Choptank River*** is a large stream. It serves Caroline,

Talbot and Dorchester counties. Ships go up the Choptank to the Port of Cambridge. Here they can use a harbor 25 feet deep. There are wharves and warehouses at the port.

The broad ***Nanticoke River*** and the ***Wicomico River*** both flow out into ***Tangier Sound.*** (Find these rivers and the Sound on your map.)

Three of our Maryland "bays" separated from the ***Atlantic Ocean*** by ***Assateague Island*** are not really bays at all. They are lagoons. A lagoon is a sheltered body of water protected by a barrier beach. Assateague Island is the barrier beach. But, we will call the lagoons ***Chincoteague, Sinepuxent,*** and ***Assawoman*** bays, since most people do! Can you find other bays in Maryland waters that we have not mentioned?

That ***ends our trip***! We have been all around Maryland on our map. We have traveled in our imaginations, not by car, boat or aircraft!

Most of Maryland's streams drain to the Atlantic Ocean.

The Water Cycle

Water travels through a never-ending cycle (circle). It falls to earth from clouds. It then returns to the air by evaporation, or can return by ***transpiration*** (being exhaled from the pores of animals or from the leaves of plants). When water evaporates or "transpires" it is in the form of an invisible water vapor (a gas). It then rises, cools and condenses out into fog or a cloud.

Do you know that fog is just a cloud resting on the surface of the ground or water? It is. As water vapor condenses even more, it becomes too heavy to stay up in the air, and falls back to earth. If the temperature is below freezing, in what form does the water come to earth? As rain? Snow? Hail or sleet?

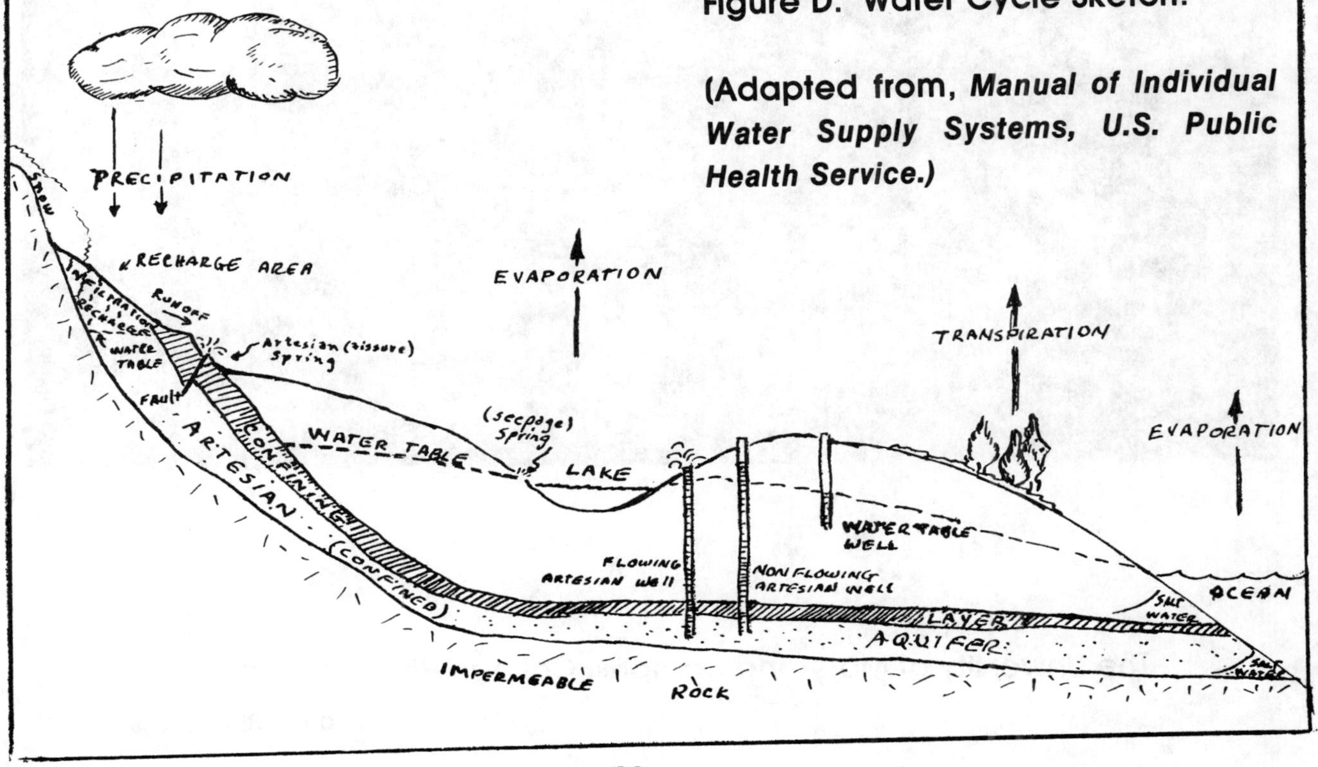

Figure D. Water Cycle Sketch.

(Adapted from, ***Manual of Individual Water Supply Systems, U.S. Public Health Service.)***

The University of Maryland campus, College Park, Maryland.

J. H. Cromwell photograph.

SECTION VI. OUR GREENERY!

The Liberty Tree, is a famous tulip poplar tree that stands on the campus of St. John's College at Annapolis.

Photograph courtesy the State of Maryland.

Native *found in and belonging to a certain place; originally from a place.*

Dinah Fiot drawing.

It is not known by many people, but the Black-eyed Susan, which grows wild now in Maryland, is not a native of Maryland. Since it grows so well here and has the black and orange colors of the Calvert family, it has been made our State Flower. (The Calvert family sent over the first Maryland colonists from England.)

Two other beautiful strangers that grow everywhere here are day-lilies and forget-me-nots.

We do have many native flowers. There are asters, goldenrod, sunflowers, wild roses, fragrant mint, clover, azaleas, rhododendron and laurel to mention just a few. Even orchids grow wild in our state! Probably not the tropical kind you are thinking of, but still, 30 different members of the orchid family. The lady-slipper is one of these.

Ferns and mosses make our woods beautiful. There is an interesting native grass here in Maryland, too. It is wild rice, often called "Indian Rice."

Berries grow beside roads and fences. First to appear in the fields in spring, are small, flavorful strawberries. Then raspberries and blackberries grow, in briary clumps, waiting to be made into pies or jams. Birds like them, too. By fall, blueberries growing near the edge of the woods are ripe.

Trees shelter Old Trinity Church at Church Creek, Dorchester County.

J. H. Cromwell photograph.

Here is our State Flower. Here is our State Tree, the White Oak. Pictures are not the same as real things, are they? For example, how tall is the flower? How tall is the tree?

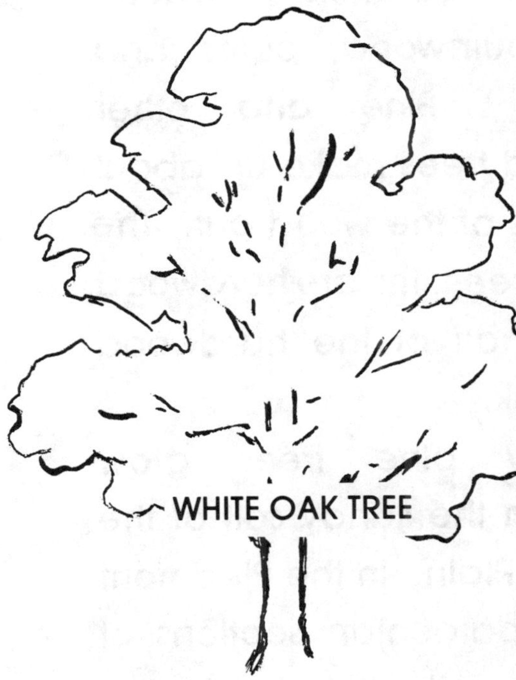

* * * * * * * * * * * *

The fine groves of trees that the first settlers saw in Maryland are gone now. New forests have grown. Much land has been cleared for homes and farming. One old giant of a tree, however, has escaped getting cut down. It is the Wye Oak at Wye Mills on the Eastern Shore. Now owned by the State of Maryland, it stands in a tiny State Park. It is a white oak tree over 400 years old. The white oak is our State Tree.

Almost half of our state is occupied by wood lots and forests.

Each year, from trees cut in our woodlands, several hundred sawmills produce posts, pulpwood, poles and pilings. Pine and other softwood trees make up about two-fifths of the wood cut. The other three-fifths are hardwood. Almost half of the hardwood cut is oak.

Loblolly pine trees grow thickly in the sandy soil of the Coastal Plain. In the Piedmont and Appalachian sections of our state, other kinds of pine trees grow.

Some of the many hardwood trees found in Maryland are: oak, red gum, tulip poplar, black locust, hickory, maple, walnut, ash and wild cherry. There are 150 different kinds of trees and large shrubs in Maryland!

The three worst dangers to our forests are insects, disease and fire. To guard our trees from fire, 34 fire lookout towers are manned during dry periods of the year. We have

Dinah Fiot drawing.

state forest rangers trained in forest fire control. They use up-to-date equipment to stop fires. Fire crews from colleges and schools help them. One of the most helpful groups in fighting forest fires is the local volunteer fire department. We citizens of the state can help. We must be very careful when we build fires. We must be certain that our fire cannot spread to the woods. We must be sure to put fires out before leaving them. We must warn people not to drop lighted cigarettes where they can cause fires.

Grazing, that is letting cattle and horses feed, in forests and wood lots can be bad for trees. The soil gets packed down. Then water cannot sink into the soil. Cattle nibbling on young trees can hurt them. Water running off hard-packed soil can cause erosion. Also, cattle eat bushes that give wildlife a place to live. Wooded slopes really should not be used for cattle grazing.

The Maryland Department of Forests and Parks helps farmers improve their woodland. Experts show farmers which trees to cut and which to plant. The woodlands can be used, we have learned, for lumber, as cover for wildlife, to conserve water, to prevent erosion, for recreation and for scenic beauty. DISCUSS THIS, PLEASE.

WORDS THAT RHYME

You will see a section of WORDS that RHYME here. Use these to help write some verses about what we have just learned.

Some of you will want to write about trees; others may choose berries, grasses or flowers. ILLUSTRATE your paper at the top with a picture. Use one you have drawn, or one you have cut out of a magazine. BELOW THE PICTURE, put the verses you have written.

Dinah Fiot Drawing.

WORDS THAT RHYME

snow, blow, show, throw, glow, mow, row, so, bow

fear, deer, here, clear, steer, near, peer, pier, dear

luck, truck, buck, tuck, duck, muck, stuck

repeat, eat, greet, beat, wheat, neat, bleat, seat

red, said, bled, dead, bed, head, thread, read, fed

grew, blew, crew, blue, do, who, knew, flew, you

pale, pail, sail, jail, wail, tale, fail, snail, gale

right, sight, light, might, bright, fight, fright, night, flight

crop, mop, hop, drop, sop, stop, shop, lop, pop

sun, run, fun, ton, done

city, pity, witty, kitty, pretty

broke, joke, poke, choke, oak, smoke, soak, woke

state, late, date, rate, gate, bait

beef, leaf, relief, reef, thief

lame, pain, shame, blame, rain, main, cane, came

boy, joy, decoy, annoy, coy, toy

fly, sky, high, sigh, by, I, pie, die, lie

stack, lack, tack, pack, rack, sack, black, back, jack

star, tar, mar, scar, car, bar, far, jar

scene, dean, bean, lean, seen, beam

WORDS THAT RHYME

brown, frown, town, down, clown

wind, blend, bend, send, end

flower, scour, sour, tower, shower

fish, wish, dish, squish, swish

maple, staple

grass, glass

cab, grab, crab

possom, blossom

cloud, loud, crowd, bowed

pearl, furl, girl, whirl, swirl, curl

ice, nice, twice, slice, rice

bird, heard, third

feather, weather, together leather

You may find many other words that rhyme. Use any words that you like to write your verses.

Near Swallow Falls in Garrett County is a unique swamp area. Here plants grow that are seldom found outside the Arctic Circle.

J. H. Cromwell photograph.

SECTION VII.

SCALES, FUR AND FEATHERS!

The Cottontail Rabbit which may be seen all year in all parts of Maryland.

Painting courtesy the Maryland Board of Natural Resources.

Amphibians	*animals that can live both on land and in water.*
Hibernate	*to sleep the winter away.*
Poisonous	*deadly; able to hurt or kill with poison.*
Reptile	*an animal that moves on its belly or on short legs, it is usually scaly.*

We have learned that wild animals must be given a place to live to survive. Sometimes they must be protected from hunters. There are no longer buffalo, wolves, elk, or passenger pigeons in our state. Almost gone, but now increasing in numbers, are wild turkey, bear, beaver, mink, wildcat and grouse.

Free Animals of the Free State

White-tailed deer roam by the thousands in woods and fields in Maryland. About 70,000 deer hunters track them each year. There are almost as many hunters as there are deer! Only about 15 out of each 100 hunters gets an animal.

Some hunters use bows and arrows. They are allowed a longer hunting season. It is hard to get a deer with a bow and arrow. Four times as many deer are accidentally killed by cars as are killed by bows and arrows. Over a thousand deer collide with automobiles each year!

The most deer are found each year in Garrett, Allegany, Cecil, Kent, Washington and Worcester counties.

Sketch by Barbara Mudd

Dinah Fiot drawing.

The ***raccoon*** is so plentiful in Maryland that he becomes a nuisance at times. He will eat almost anything. His fur is thick, grey and black, with white marks. It is quite a valuable skin. Across his pointed nose and around his eyes is a black "mask." Like a monkey, the little raccoon is friendly and curious.

Cottontail rabbits, too, are found all over our state. They are our most hunted animals.

The ***red fox*** and the ***grey fox*** are found in all our counties. The grey fox hunts at night, so is not seen as often as the red fox. The red fox is the smarter of the two. He is more of a daytime animal. He does not seem to mind living near people. The red fox is a beautiful animal about the size of a small dog. His rich fur is red and his feet are black. His clever nose is sharp and his ears are pointed. He has a bushy, white-tipped tail.

Squirrels and ***chipmunks*** do well all over Maryland. These pretty little animals eat fruit, buds, insects and nuts. They live in trees. Not seen too often is our flying squirrel. He can glide as far as 150 feet from a tree 60 feet high!

The ***woodchuck*** is also called a "groundhog." It lives all around the state and likes open country. It is one of the few animals in our state that really hibernates. This brown-grey animal weighs about six to twelve pounds. It is not very pretty, but it doesn't seem to mind.

An ***opossum*** will pretend that it is dead when something bothers it. Have you heard your mother or father say that you are "playing 'possum" when you snuggle deeper into your bed on winter mornings?

The opossum is a very interesting animal. It eats any small bird or animal or insect it can get. The mother keeps her babies in a pouch, warm and safe, until they grow large. She sometimes lets her young ones ride around on her back. The opossum has a long, bare, funny tail. The opossum thinks this tail is very nice, however, for it helps it to climb trees more easily.

Dinah Fiot drawing.

Mink live along Maryland waterways. They are not easily seen. They are very wild. The mink is a long, beautiful little animal with wonderful, shiny fur. They can be raised in captivity. Though only about two feet long, tail and all, they are fierce fighters.

Dinah Fiot drawing.

The ***otter,*** like the little mink, can travel long distances. The otter lives beside and in the water. They eat fish. The ***beaver*** is another Maryland animal that likes to live in and near water. The number of beaver is increasing today. The beaver likes to build a dam across a stream. There in a safe chamber, the beaver family can live snugly and safely.

Dinah Fiot Drawing.

The *weasel* is a hunter! It kills thousands of mice, rats and even rabbits. In turn, the weasel is hunted by owls, house cats and hawks. It is said to kill just for the love of it! It is not a very lovable animal, is it? The weasel is long, with short legs. The fur is dark brown on top, tan or white beneath.

Skunks are found all around our state. They are also called a "woods pussy," or a "polecat." They are very pretty animals with soft black fur. A large white stripe runs from the head to the tail. It is not very popular with humans, however. Do you know why?

Reptiles found in Maryland are lizards, snakes and turtles.

Only two of our 26 kinds of snake are poisonous. These two are the copperhead and the timber rattlesnake. They are mostly found in rocky, mountainous areas. They like to sleep in the day and hunt for mice and rats at night.

Turtles of twelve different kinds travel (slowly) around in Maryland. Once in a while a big ocean turtle will visit Chesapeake Bay.

Loved by children are the

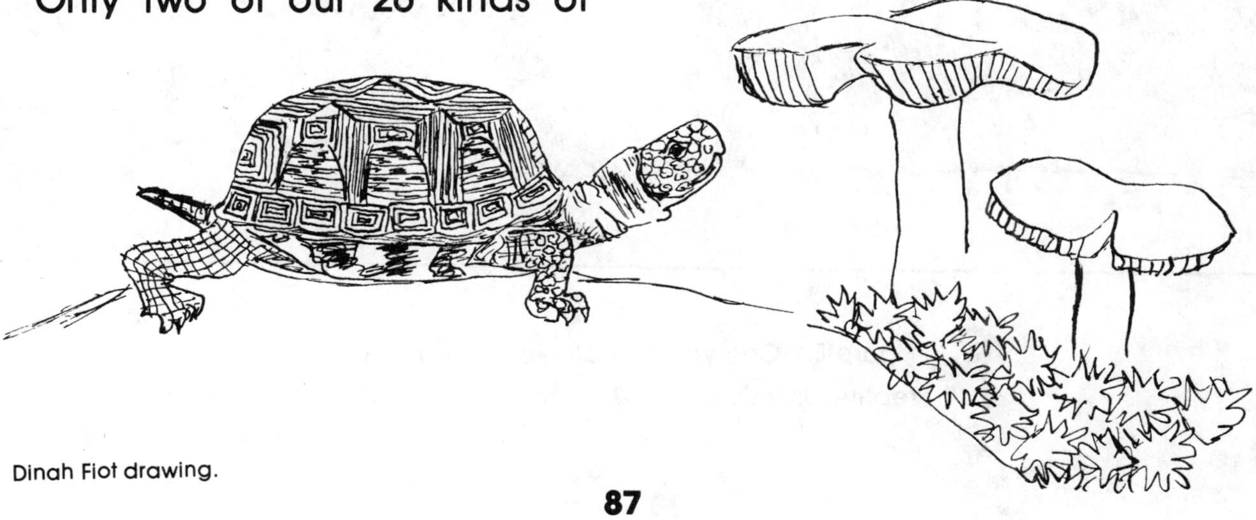

Dinah Fiot drawing.

little reptiles that can live on land or in water. These are called "amphibians." You say it, "am-fib-ee-annes." These favorite pets are frogs, salamanders and toads.

Before we go on to learn about Maryland fish and birds, will you see if you can find the animals and reptiles we have hidden in the picture (Figure E)? GOOD HUNTING . .

Figure E. Can you find all ***ten*** animals and reptiles in this picture?

The Great Snowy Owl.

Painting by John W. Taylor, courtesy the Maryland Board of Natural Resources.

Free Birds of the Free State

What good is a bird?

Birds are beautiful to see. They are nice to hear. But, birds are also very useful to us for another reason. They eat tons of insects each year. Also, game birds and waterfowl are good to eat! Our birds are very useful. Yes, even the big, ugly turkey buzzard is a useful bird. What does he do for us?

Our State Bird is the orange and black, ***Baltimore Oriole.*** As in our State Flower, the Black-eyed Susan, the colors are those of the Calvert family.

Dinah Fiot drawing.

★★★★★★★★★★★★★★★★★★★★★★★★

Migrate *travel a regular path each year.*

★★★★★★★★★★★★★★★★★★★★★★★★

As we have said before, this English family was the one to send colonists to Maryland from England. The head of the family at that time was the second Lord Baltimore. The birds named for Lord Baltimore's family title are about eight inches long. They spend summers in Maryland. In the winters they live in Mexico and Central America!

Game birds are hunted for food. Maryland duck is famous. It makes a very fine dinner! There are 25 or more kinds of duck, geese and swan that live in Maryland. Some migrate into the state. Many stop here to rest on their way north in the summer, or south in the winter. Our waterfowl live on open waters, in marshes, and along shallow waterways. There are several wildlife refuges in Maryland. Here they can live without being hunted.

Other game birds are ***quail, grouse, pheasant,*** and though fewer in number, ***wild turkeys*** and ***mourning doves.*** Most of the wild turkeys are to be found in the western part of our state. Game birds need shelter in bushes and weeds.

Dinah Fiot drawing.

Songbirds should never be hunted. Just to name some of our Maryland songbirds is a pleasure. Listen to these names! Living in Maryland are the mockingbird, cardinal, song sparrow, bluebird, blue jay, meadowlark, flicker, wren, kingfisher, Maryland yellow-throat, red-winged blackbird, tufted titmouse, and of course, our well-loved robins.

Speaking of birds, the ***Great American Bald Eagle*** is found beside Chesapeake Bay and along the Potomac River. It is getting quite rare. When the eagle eats fish and small animals that have chemicals on them, it can be harmed. Chemicals used to kill weeds and to control insects are not good for the eagle.

The Eastern Bluebird.

John W. Taylor painting. Courtesy Md. Board of Natural Resources.

CHOOSE TWO OR THREE BIRDS.

Find out something about them. Write two verses on each bird. You may find that some of the words that rhyme in Section VI will help.

Game Fish

Fishermen by the thousands go to our mountain counties to fish for trout. Other thousands come to the Bay, the ocean and our rivers to fish for our many game fish.

Marlin, cod, bonita, sea herring, porgy, mackeral, whiting, sturgeon, bluefish, all of these like ocean waters. Fish that like fast-running rivers are the black bass, trout, and catfish. The alewife, also called menhaden, is caught in large numbers. Some fish like only warm water. Some of these are bass, sunfish, crappies, perch, pickeral, suckers and eel.

Some small fish are called minnows. Though not big enough to eat, they are very important fish. Minnows are a link in the "chain of life." They eat insects and worms; then larger fishes eat them.

Once in a while a porpoise will visit Chesapeake Bay. The porpoise is sometimes called the "clown of the Chesapeake."

Dinah Fiot drawing.

The Chesapeake Bay Retriever is shown here leaping into the water to bring back game.

Courtesy Maryland Board of Natural Resources.

Painting by J. M. Roever.

SECTION VIII.

MARYLAND MINING

The Baltimore skyline in 1972 as the USF§G Building was under construction. Much Maryland stone and Maryland-made bricks are needed in construction in Baltimore City. Much sand and gravel is used in making new buildings, homes and roadways.

J. H. Comwell photograph.

We have some very interesting metals in Maryland. Few are plentiful enough to pay us to mine them. We have gold, silver, chromium, iron, copper and other metals.

Our stone, which does not seem at first glance to be very valuable, is! The quarrying of sand, gravel and building stone produces income in Maryland. Many tons of gravel and crushed rock are needed to build our highways, homes and big buildings. Our Maryland building stones are---marble, limestone and granite. These are quarried out in large blocks and slabs.

Clay, which makes good building brick, is found in Maryland. Several brick-yards are busy in our state. In Western Maryland "fire clay," is mined. This clay makes a kind of brick that can stand a lot of heat. It does not conduct heat as much as other clays do, because of its low metal content. It is used to line furnaces and chimneys which have to stand very high temperatures.

Coal mining used to be an important work in Western Maryland. Then, for years, little was mined. The coal which was easiest to reach was used up. The use of cheap oil and natural gas made coal unpopular as a fuel. Now, however, coal is again becoming an important fuel.

There is plenty of coal still in the ground in Maryland. It is fairly expensive to mine.

Though there has been no oil discovered in Maryland, there are producing, natural gas wells. These are located in the Mountain Lake Park and the Accident areas of Western Maryland.

Gas drilling rigs are shown here.

Courtesy Washington Gas Light Co.

SECTION IX.
POPULATION FACTS

Townhouses are often handsome and conserve land and energy. These have south-facing windows that collect winter sunshine.

Sketch courtesy the U. S. Department of Energy.

Census *a count. Each ten years the United States takes a census. All of the people are counted.*
Population *people; or, people belonging to one place.*
Suburb *land outside a town or city where many people live.*

1. SHOWING OFF OUR "POP FAX"

Do you know that YOU are a part of the state population now? Yes. You are a ***very important*** part. You will be doing all kinds of work in the interesting years ahead. Of all the treasures a state can have, the most valuable is---its boys and girls.

Maryland in recent years, grew faster than most states in our nation in population. The 1970 and the 1980 census showed that there are more boys than girls growing up in Maryland. In 1980 there were about 108,000 boys, and about 105,000 girls, less than five years old, living in Maryland.

Maryland ranks 18th in population of all the states.

About one-third of all the people in Maryland live in Baltimore City and Baltimore County. In fact, about one-half the people in the state live in, or near, Baltimore City!

* *

Population Facts for Maryland

Census	
1950	2 1/3 million people
1960	3 1/5 million people
1970	3 9/10 million people
1980	4 1/5 million people

* *

EXERCISE

To SHOW how Maryland has grown, in population, we are going to make a graph. This can also show how many people will be living here in the years ahead!

Using the facts shown in the table above, use a blank sheet of paper. Make a graph like the one on the page following this one. Draw columns up over the years.

We want to make a graph that will:

(a) Show the number of people living in Maryland in 1950. Color this column RED.

(b) Show the number of people here in 1960 by a BLUE column.

(c) Next show the number of people here in 1970 with a WHITE column.

(d) Now show the number of people here in 1980 with an ORANGE column.

(e) Show how many people may live in Maryland in 1990! To find this number, let's pretend that the next 10 years of growth will be the same as the last ten. In the last ten years Maryland gained about 3/10 of a million people. Color your 1990 column GREEN. This will show future growth and progress in Maryland.

OUR MARYLAND POPULATION
1950 TO 1990

People

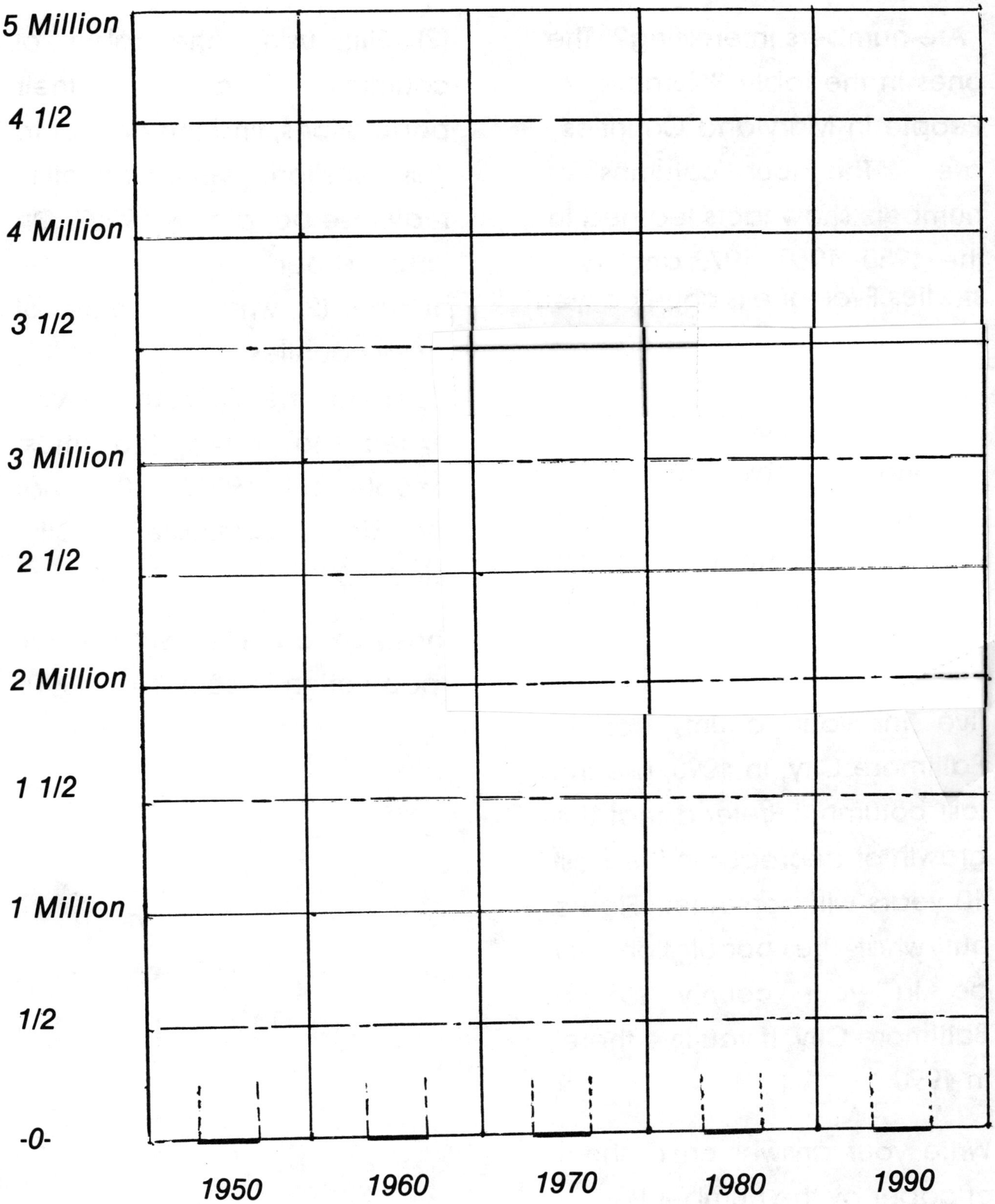

2. MARYLAND COUNTIES 1950 to 1990

Are numbers interesting? The ones in the table "Number of People in Maryland Counties" are. The four columns of numbers show facts learned in the 1950, 1960, 1970 and 1980 studies.Everyone is counted, you know, each ten years. There are plans to "take a census," that is, to count everyone, more often. Each five years might be the new plan.

Exercise.

To see how many people will live in your county, or in Baltimore City, in 1990, use the last column. Pretend that the growth or decrease in the past 10 years will continue. Figure out what the population will be in your county (or in Baltimore City, if you live there) in 1990.

Write your answer on a sheet of paper by the number (1).

(2) Still using the table of counties and their populations, find the answer to this question. Which counties may lose people by 1990? On your sheet of paper, by number (2), write the names of these counties.

(3) Name the six counties you expect to have the most people by 1990. (Do not include Baltimore City, please.)

These six counties will be our "population leaders" by 1990!

Number of People in Maryland Counties

County	People Counted 1950	People Counted 1960	People Counted 1970	People Counted 1980	Last 10 years--- Percent of change
Baltimore City	949,708	939,024	905,787	783,320	−13.5
Allegany	89,556	84,169	84,044	80,413	− 4.3
Anne Arundel	117,392	206,634	298,042	369,914	+24.1
Baltimore	270,273	492,428	620,409	651,105	+ 4.9
Calvert	12,100	15,826	20,682	34,308	+65.9
Caroline	18,234	19,462	19,781	23,148	+17.0
Carroll	44,907	52,785	69,006	96,056	+39.2
Cecil	33,356	48,408	53,291	60,113	+12.8
Charles	23,415	32,572	47,678	72,343	+51.7
Dorchester	27,815	29,666	29,405	30,549	+ 3.9
Frederick	62,287	71,930	84,927	111,687	+31.5
Garrett	21,259	20,420	21,476	26,502	+23.4
Harford	51,782	76,722	115,378	145,592	+26.2
Howard	23,119	36,152	62,394	118,443	+89.8
Kent	13,677	15,481	16,146	16,680	+ 3.3
Montgomery	164,401	340,928	522,809	574,106	+ 9.8
Prince George's	194,182	357,395	661,719	657,707	− 0.6
Queen Anne's	14,579	16,569	18,422	25,520	+38.5
St. Mary's	29,111	38,915	47,388	59,799	+26.2
Somerset	20,745	19,623	18,924	19,041	+ 0.6
Talbot	19,428	21,578	23,682	25,496	+ 7.7
Washington	78,886	91,219	103,829	112,764	+ 8.6
Wicomico	39,641	49,050	54,236	64,979	+19.8
Worcester	23,148	23,733	24,442	30,303	+24.0
TOTAL MARYLAND POPULATION			3,923,897	4,193,378	+6.9

Baltimore County Court House (1969 photograph).

J. H. Cromwell photograph.

3. SOME MARYLAND COMMUNITIES

Here are the names of several Maryland communities. Some have no city government of thier own.

These are called ***unincorporated*** places. The county they are in gives them fire and police protection, government and other services. These places have a "U" beside them.

These are, of course, only a few of Maryland's communities. There are many, many more. Census booklets on Maryland will give them all.

A greenhouse added to a standard house can save energy. It can be a cool, shaded place in summer and in the winter can collect heat from the sun.

Sketch courtesy the U.S. Department of Energy.

Place Name and County	1970 Population	1980 Population
Annapolis (A.A.)	30,100	31,400
Balt. City	906,000	783,300
Bowie (P.G.)	35,000	33,700
College Park (P.G.)	26,200	23,700
Columbia "U" (Howard)	8,815	52,400
Cumberland (Allegany)	29,700	26,000
Denton (Caroline)	1,600	1,900
Frederick (Fred.)	23,600	25,100
Hagerstown (Washington)	35,900	34,100
Leonardtown (St. Mary's)	1,400	1,400
Rockville *(Montgomery)*	42,700	43,600
Salisbury (Wicomico)	15,300	16,300
Silver Spring "U" (Montgomery)	77,400	71,100
Towson "U" (Baltimore)	77,800	50,800
Wheaton-Glenmont "U" (Montgomery)	66,300	48,500

4. A "POP FAX" QUIZ ON MARYLAND COMMUNITIES

Take a sheet of paper and write the numbers one through nine down the left side.

Put your answers to the questions below, by your numbers.

(1) By adding the number of people in Baltimore City, 1980, to the number living nearby in Baltimore County, 1980, you will find that ***many*** people live in Baltimore City and Baltimore County. What number do you get? That is a large number! And just think, we are not even adding the people living in the other nearby counties!

(2) If 4,193,378 people lived in Maryland in 1980, does the number you found in question (1) tell us about 1/3 or 1/4 of Maryland's people live in Baltimore City and Baltimore County? (Again, we are not even adding in other nearby counties.)

About what fraction (or per cent) of the population of Maryland is this?

(3) Maryland areas near two big U.S. cities grow faster in population than do other Maryland locations. What are the names of these two big cities?

(4) Look at our list of Maryland places. Name the places that lost people between 1970 and 1980.

POP FAX QUIZ

(5) Look again at the list and see what place grew 600 percent, in just 10 years!
(a) Name this community.
(b) Give a reason for its growth.

(6) (a) List the Maryland communities that have over 50,000 people. (b) Are these places near Baltimore City or Washington, D.C.?

(7) ***Most*** people decide to move because (pick one) they can: (a) raise chickens; (b) get a better job; (c) get nice weather.

(8) An ***incorporated*** town is one with a government that is separate from the county government. Is this true or false?

(9) A ***suburb*** is an area near a city or town where many people live. Is this true or false?

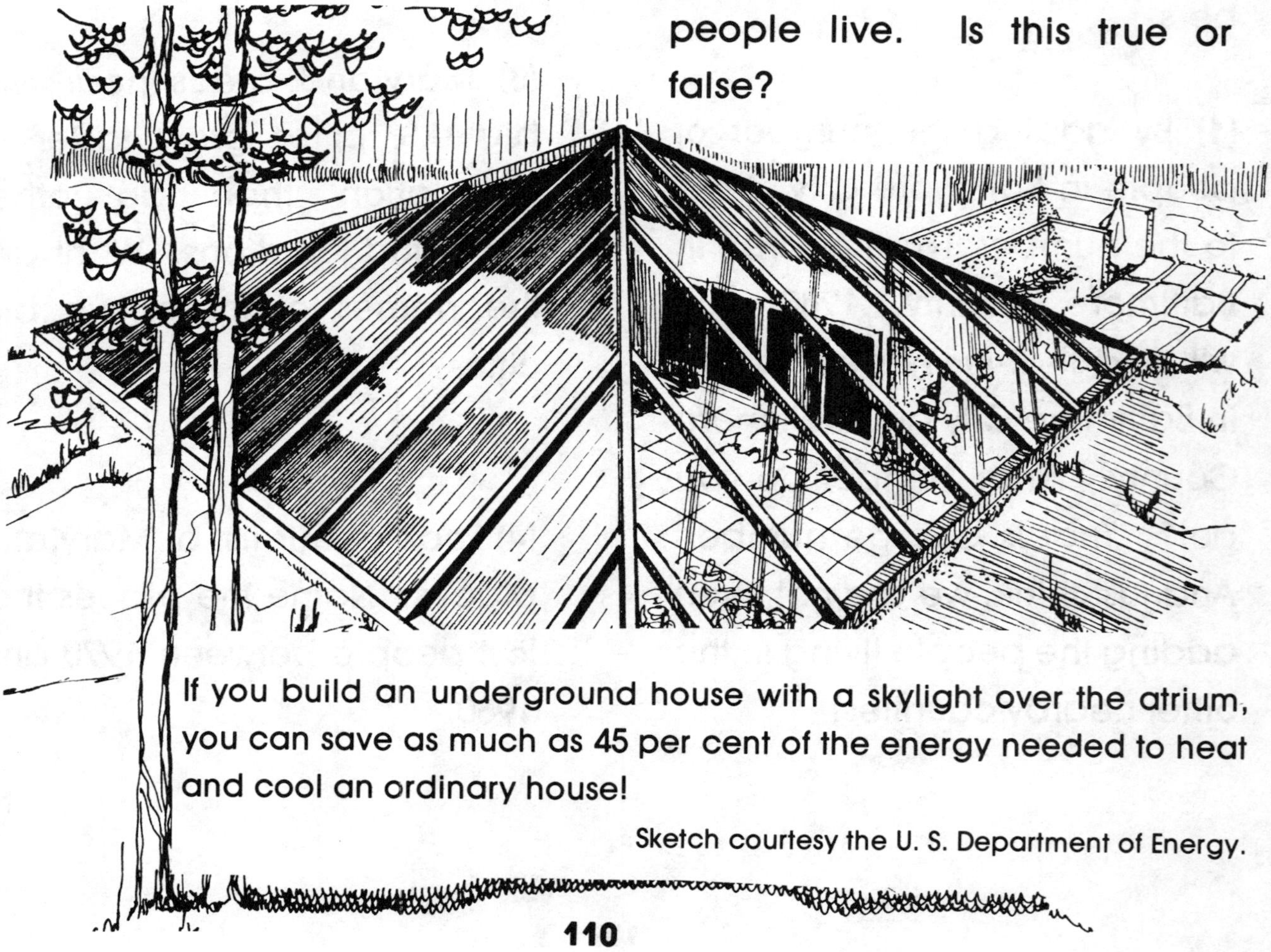

If you build an underground house with a skylight over the atrium, you can save as much as 45 per cent of the energy needed to heat and cool an ordinary house!

Sketch courtesy the U. S. Department of Energy.

SECTION X.
WHAT KIND OF WORK DOES A MARYLAND WORKER DO?

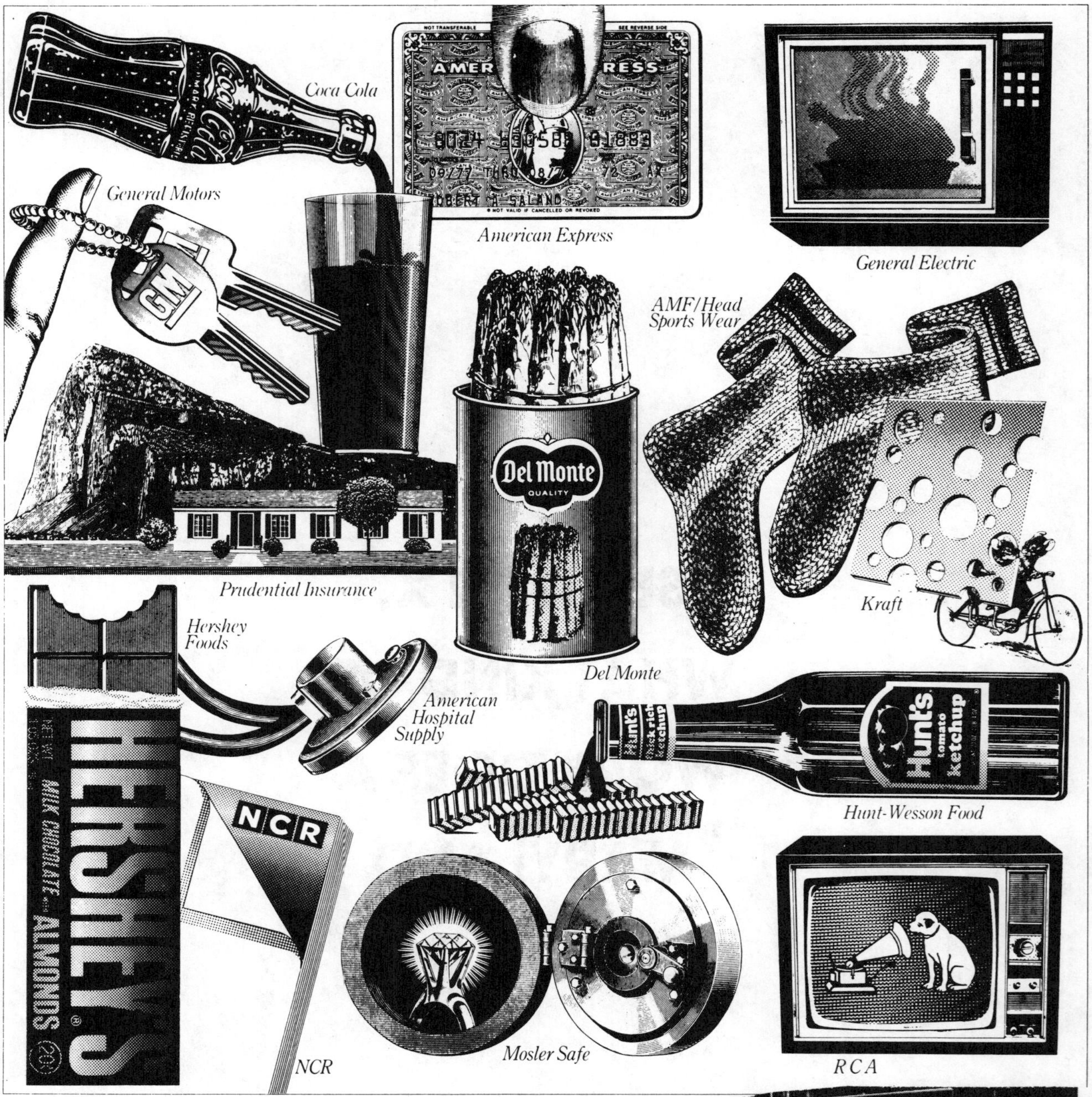
Coca Cola
General Motors
American Express
General Electric
AMF/Head Sports Wear
Prudential Insurance
Del Monte
Kraft
Hershey Foods
American Hospital Supply
Hunt-Wesson Food
NCR
Mosler Safe
RCA
HERSHEY'S
MILK CHOCOLATE
ALMONDS
Hunt's
tomato
ketchup

NCR
CENTURY

1. A LOOK INTO THE FUTURE

When a country is first settled, most of its people may work at PRIMARY work. That is, a work which takes things right from the land. Mining, farming, fishing and lumbering are good examples of primary work.

Later, people begin to do SECONDARY kinds of work. They manufacture things (make things).

Finally, as a country grows older, people go into SERVICE work. This might be government, tourism, dry cleaning or restaurant work.

Maryland has done this. We used to be an ***agricultural*** state. Later we made most of our money from ***manufacturing. Soon*** most of our money will come from work which ***serves*** people.

Before we find out what kind of work there is to do right now, let's peer ahead into the future! What kind of work will there be to do when you are grown?

Two new kinds of work which are growing very fast in Maryland are:

(1) ***Research and development.*** Men and women in these jobs invent many things. They find out new things. They have new ideas. When they invent a machine, they may build a few to show how it can be done.

(2) ***Tourism.*** More and more tourists are coming to Maryland. Intelligent and energetic people are needed to work for hotels, stores, motels, and all the many places tourists like. Can you

think of some other jobs that would help entertain tourists?

Employment in Maryland

Total number of persons employed in 1976—1,541,500

	Number of Employees
Government	371,900
Wholesale & Retail Trade	362,300
Community, Social, & Personal Services	288,000
Manufacturing	231,600
Construction	93,700
Finance, Insurance, & Real Estate	80,100
Transportation & Public Utilities	78,100
Agriculture & Mining	35,800

Sources: *Employment and Earnings*, September 1977, U.S. Bureau of Labor Statistics; *Farm Labor*, February 1977, U.S. Department of Agriculture.

In the future, we will find ***manufacturing*** strong, still growing.

Farming will be needed and still important. It will use fewer people. Also, it will earn a little less of the total money made in Maryland. About half of our Maryland land is now farmland. Yet, less than three out of each 100 workers, work in agriculture! DISCUSS this interesting fact.

Education. Almost 1/3 of our state budget is spent on education today. It will still be very much needed when you are grown.

Government. In the past 15 years, the money-making work that grew more than any other kind was government! This kind of work will keep on growing, though not so fast as before. Today, about 20 out of each 100 Maryland workers are in government jobs. There are national, state, county and local governments.

2. KINDS OF WORK DONE TODAY

You will find many unexpected things in the list on the next page. It will tell you how many people work, and what they do, in Maryland. This information comes from the census studies and from our Maryland data offices.

EMPLOYMENT IN MARYLAND

(In 1980 there were over 1,900,000 workers in Maryland.)

Jobs, in thousands	0 50 100 150 200 250 300 350 400
MANUFACTURING	★★★★★★★★★★★★★★★★★★★
FARMING, FISHING, FORESTRY	★★
MINING	★
BUILDING	★★★★★★★
TRANSPORTATION	★★★★★★
SALES, SELLING	★★★★★★★★★★★★★★★★★★★★★★★★★★★★★★
FINANCE (BANKS), INSURANCE REAL ESTATE	★★★★★★
PERSONAL SERVICES	★★★★★
ENTERTAINMENT AND RECREATION	★★★
PROFESSIONAL AND OTHER SERVICES	★★★★★★★★★★★★★★★★★★★★★★★
GOVERNMENT	★★★★★★★★★★★★★★★★★★★★★★★★★★
OTHER WORK NOT REPORTED	★★★★★★★

(Much of the data on this and the following pages was obtained from the State of Maryland, Department of Economic and Community Development and the U.S. Department of Commerce, Bureau of the Census.)

***Figure 6. KINDS OF WORK THAT MARYLAND WORKERS DID IN** 1980.*

Workers are shown tapping trees to gather maple syrup. These maple trees are near Oakland, Maryland.

J. H. Cromwell photograph.

EXERCISE

Using the bar graph shown, and following the EXAMPLE given, make your own list on a piece of paper. Make a list of OCCUPATIONS. Leave a left margin of about an inch in width. In the top space, put the name of the kind of work done by the greatest number of people. On the second line put the next largest occupation, and so on, down to the smallest. JUST WRITE ENOUGH to tell what you mean, not the whole name of the work. (Example: Mfg. for manufacturing.)

(B) Now, in the margin space you have to the LEFT, for each occupation, write ***P*** if it is Primary; or a 2 is it is Secondary, or an ***S*** if it is Service work. (Example: On the left of "Finance" you would put the letter ***S***.)

P ***Primary***

2 ***Secondary***

S ***Service***

MAKING THINGS (MANUFACTURING)!

As we have just seen, a very large group of working people are busy making things, manufacturing things, in Maryland.

What do they make? To get an idea, look at the graph "People Working In Maryland Manufacturing."

One of the largest kinds of manufacturing in our state is that of making metals from ore. (Ore, you know is rock, dirt or sand that contains metals.)

Another very big manufacturing business is preparing foods for sale.

Can you see why Baltimore leads in both kinds of manufacturing? It is because there are good, deep-water channels coming into Baltimore City which ocean-going ships can use to bring ore to the metal-working mills.

Good railroads, too, serve Baltimore City.

Fine highways are ready for big trucks to use to carry food from anywhere in our state. All over Maryland there are food processing plants, cooking, canning, and freezing food to sell! The ships, trains, and trucks then carry the processed metals and foods away---off to market!

Skilled Maryland workers make trucks, busses, boxcars and trailers. Others are at work making clothing for men, women and children.

Other people are busy at making hundreds of items from metal and from paper. Busy, too, are the workers in plants that make chemicals and things from chemicals.

Going down the list of manufacturing work done in our state, we see that some workers make electrical machinery. Some print books. Others publish books and newspapers.

Still other workers make machinery that is not run by electrical motors. Some work at making things of stone, clay and glass. Some people work at making items from paper pulp. Some make furniture, cloth, shoes and prepare lumber for use.

What a ***lot of things*** are made in Maryland!

The Washington Monument in Baltimore City.

J. H. Cromwell photograph.

PEOPLE WORKING IN MARYLAND MANUFACTURING

(In 1978 a total of 242,000 people worked in manufacturing.)

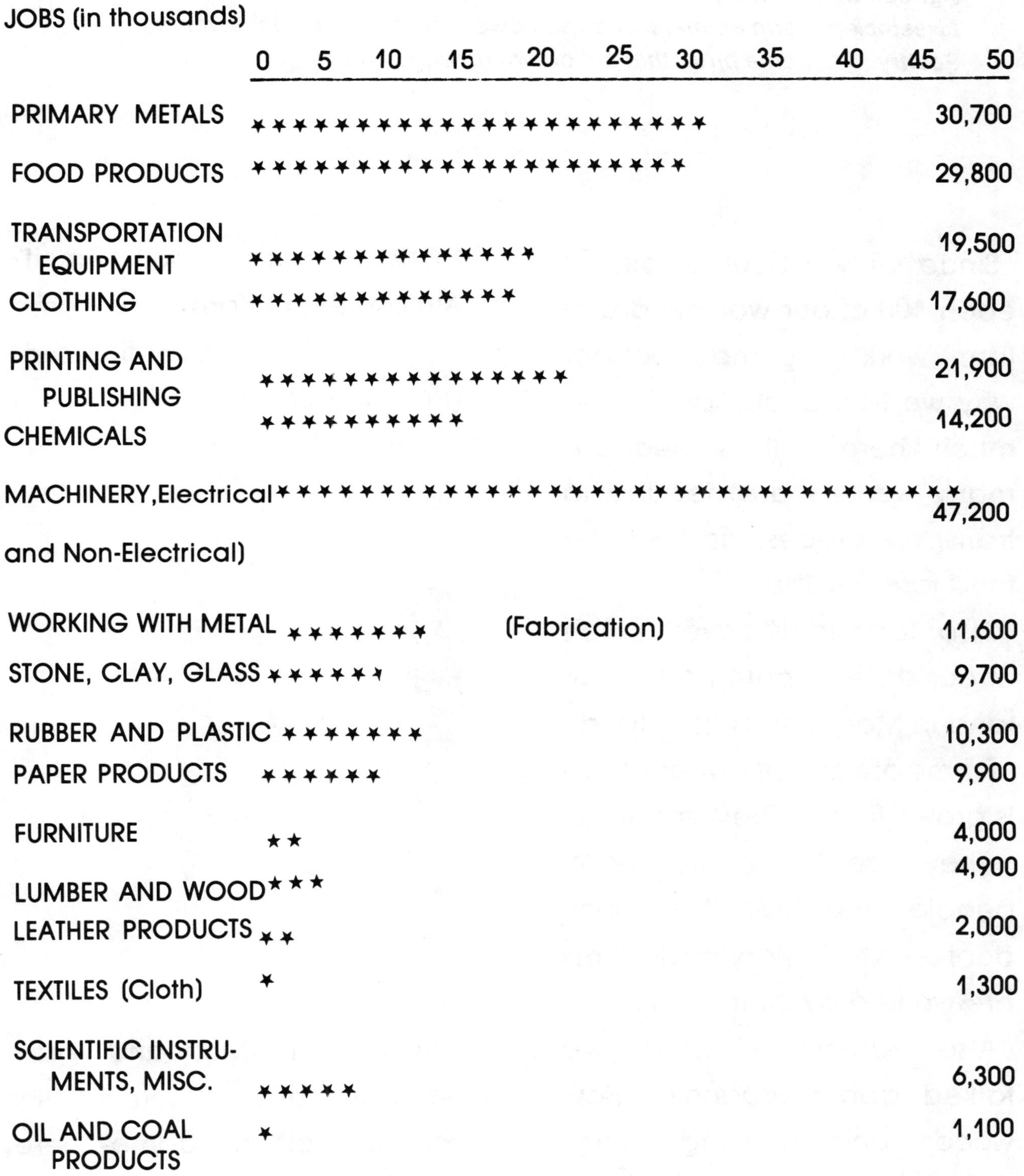

Figure 7. People Working in Maryland Manufacturing, 1978.

3. FARMING

Agriculture *farming.*
Livestock *farm animals, such as cows, horses, pigs, sheep, mules.*
Poultry *tame birds that are grown for eggs and meat.*

Since only about 3 out of each 100 of our workers are in farm work, you may wonder why we talk about farming so much here. It is because many workers are needed to transport, process and sell the food farmers raise.

Also, farm land covers much of our state. About half of our land in Maryland is farm land.

Farms are places where food is grown for us. They are more.

They are homes to many people who love the out-of-doors. Most Maryland farms are worked by their owners.

Also, remember when we talked about erosion? How woods and growing things slow rain and snow down so that the water does not rush off to rivers carrying soil with it? Almost every farm has some woods. They have fields of growing things.

Indians in Maryland grew several crops. When the first English settlers came here, crops had to be planted right away. (Why was this?)

Until the Civil War, Maryland workers were mostly employed on farms. Today, more people work in office work, manufacturing and scientific work. Still, we need our farms. They do much for us.

As you might guess, today the way to make money from a farm is to grow things that can be used by people in nearby towns and cities. So, we should not be a bit surprised to find ***dairy farming*** Maryland's largest farm business. Milk and the sale of poultry make up about 2/3 of all farm sales! Poultry raised for market in Maryland includes chickens and turkeys.

The other 1/3 of the money made on farms is from selling crops. Maryland is important as a state whose workers pack, freeze and can meat, seafood and vegetables. Tons of food are also taken right to market from the fields, to be sold as fresh produce.

Vegetables Grown In Our State

We are off on a WORD HUNT! There are eleven vegetables that make the most money for farmers in Maryland. YOU have to find out what they are from our WORD HUNT HINTS. The most important vegetable is listed in Hint (1); the least valuable income crop of the eleven is listed last. On a sheet of paper, write the numbers (1) through (11). Write the name of the vegetables described in the hints beside your numbers.

A WORD HUNT

(1) I'm American. Indians grew me. I am also called "maize."

(2) I'm all red. You can eat me raw or cooked. I make nice salads, sauces and soups. I am used in making catsup.

(3) I am a bean that goes "snap" when broken.

(4) I am a kind of pea. I am served at banquets with chicken, and am often in TV dinners.

(5) I'm green and cool as a cucumber. I am often found in salads and in pickle factories.

(6) I am a yam. You can eat me as a vegetable dish or make me into a pie.

(7) I am a potato named for a European people, but I was first found in South America.

(8) I am eaten with a sauce of cheese or a white sauce. I'm green. My name rhymes with the words, "pass-their-bus."

(9) I'm nice in summer. Pink and red inside, I am deep green outside. You can drink the first part of my name.

(10) I'm a nice bean. I'm pale green. The city for which I'm named is in South America. Llamas live there.

(11) I am orange inside, tan and green outside. I stay in my fields until picked, for I can't elope with anyone.

What Grows Where?

Just as our land, climate, and ways of earning money are varied---so are our farms. Most farmers in Maryland grow several things (some of this, some of that).

The Western Maryland farmer will probably raise livestock. He, or she, may grow potatoes, buckwheat or oats. The farmer might cut and sell timber, too. In springtime maple trees may be "tapped" and the syrup that is gathered will be sold. Apples and peaches, grow well in many Maryland orchards.

The farmer in the North-Central part of the state may have a dairy herd and also raise beef cattle. The farmer is likely to have chickens and other poultry. In the fields, grain, hay and fodder is grown to feed the cattle and other livestock.

Eastern Shore farmers have found that raising chickens is very profitable. You might say that there has been a "broiler boom" there! They also grow all sorts of vegetables and grains in the light soils. Some find it a good idea to make money with milk cows and to raise beef cattle. Often, an Eastern Shore farmer is also a "waterman." When he is not busy farming, he gathers seafood to make money.

Dinah Fiot Drawing.

A tobacco barn in Southern Maryland. Notice openings which help ventilate tobacco hung inside.

J. H. Cromwell photograph.

A farmer in Southern Maryland will almost certainly raise a field or two of fine Maryland tobacco. The farmers raise it, "cure" it, and take it to Upper Marlboro or to Hughesville, where it can be sold by auction. (Ask your teacher to explain the word "auction.")

Then, too, the Southern Maryland farmer may raise livestock on the farm. Also, grains and vegetables are often grown there.

USING THE GRAPH (Figure 8), list the 10 farm products that earn the most money for our Maryland farmers. List the ***best*** money-maker ***first,*** then the second best and so on down the list. Thank you.

CROPS AND LIVESTOCK SOLD IN

MARYLAND

APPROXIMATE VALUE IN DOLLARS 1977

(Sales in millions of dollars.)

The 1977 total was over $675 million.

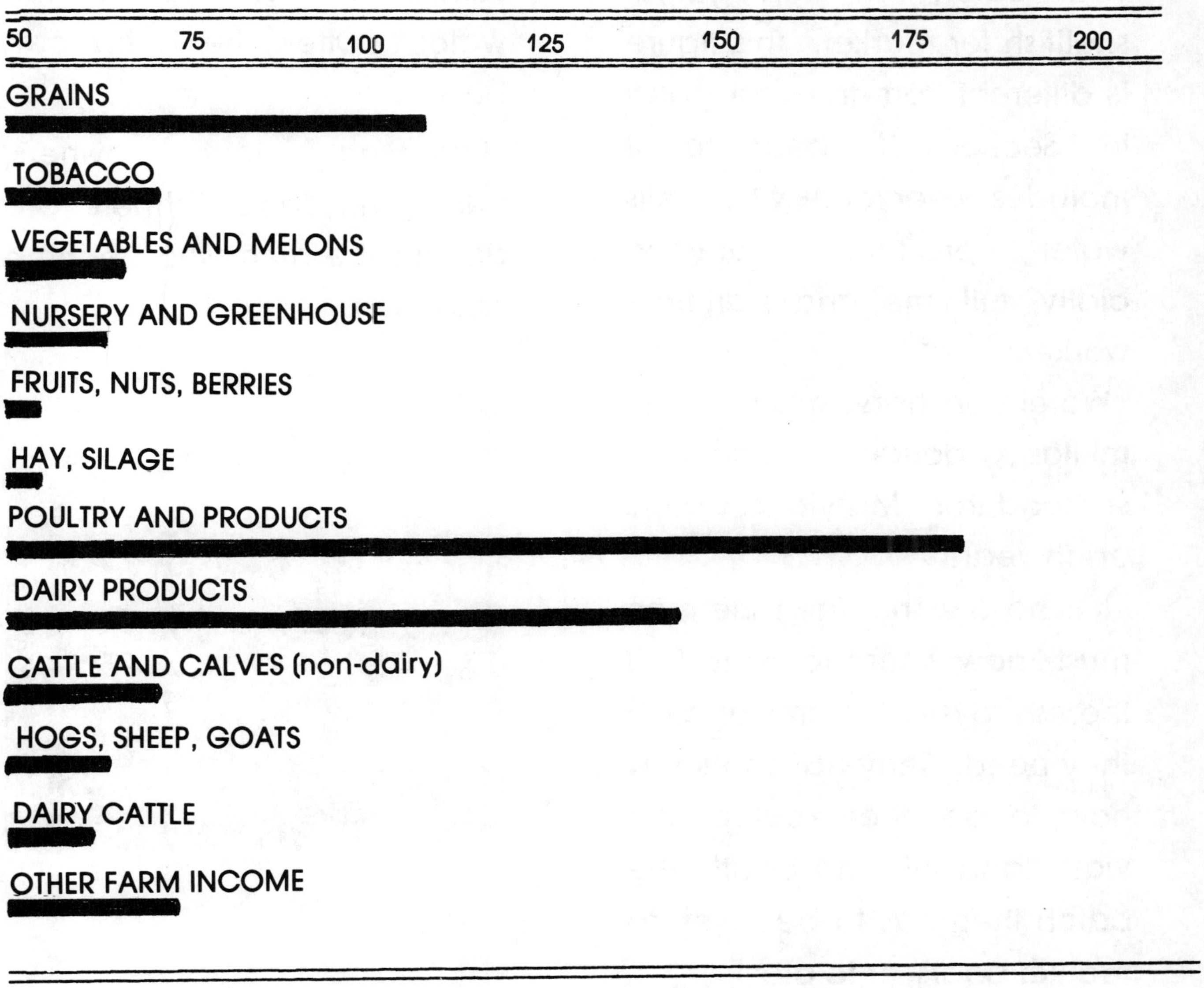

Figure 8. Graph showing dollar value of Maryland farm products.

Shellfish *clams, oysters, crabs.*

★★★★★★★★★★★★★★★★★★★★★★★★

4. WATERMEN

The number of men who work on Maryland waters does not change much from year to year. About 16,000 men each year catch fish and gather shellfish for market. This figure is different from the one given in Section X, because it includes everyone who sells water products commercially, full-time and part-time workers.

Watermen harvest over thirty million dollars worth of seafood from Maryland waters each year.

It is hard work. The fishermen must know where to go to find the fish, oysters, clams or crab they need. They have to know how to get them out of the water and into the boat! The catch then has to be taken to market boats, or to piers.

A waterman must also be wise in the ways of the weather. He has to stand hot sun, bitter cold, wet, wind, and long hours of work. But, he isn't afraid of work! He likes being outside. He finds much satisfaction working on the water. Often, he is his own boss.

Professors, land owners, merchants, and farmers are among the men who become fishermen.

OYSTERS are our most valuable water "crop" in Maryland. The Chesapeake Bay is the largest oyster-growing area in the world. Each year about fifteen million dollars are earned from the sale of oysters.

CLAMS and CRABS earn watermen over twenty million dollars each year. (The clams are about as valuable to fishermen as the crabs are.)

Compare the amount of money made by watermen with that made by farmers. To do this, use the graph below when you have finished it. Compare it with the farm graph in Figure 8.

DRAW A GRAPH like the example shown below. SHOW the amount of money made by the sale of oysters, finfish, crabs and clams. (Extend the black bars.)

EXAMPLE

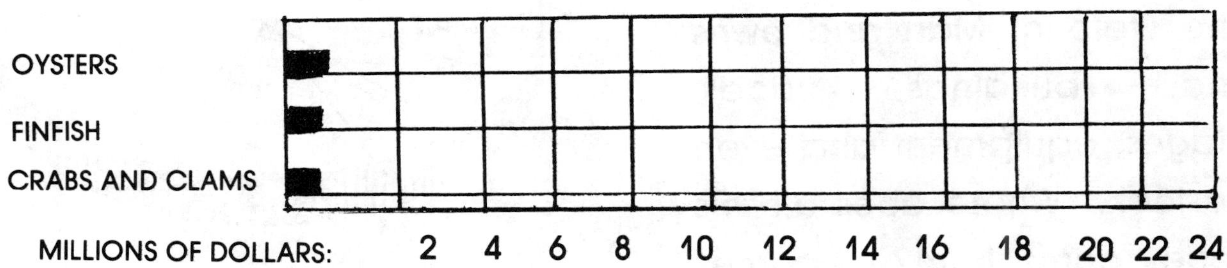

5. GOVERNMENT WORK

★★★

*The United States government is also called our **federal government.***

★★★

State government in Maryland gives us our roads, health services, police protection, schools, colleges and many other services each year. The government of Maryland must spend large amounts of money. Have you every wondered how much money?

Each year, Maryland's government collects, and then spends, over ***four billion dollars***!

The State of Maryland owns land, buildings, roads, bridges, equipment and even livestock. Where does all this money come from? It comes from several kinds of taxes, fees, and from some federal payments. DISCUSS this last sentence to be sure you know what all the words mean, please.

Our state has a law that each year its budget must be balanced. What does this mean?

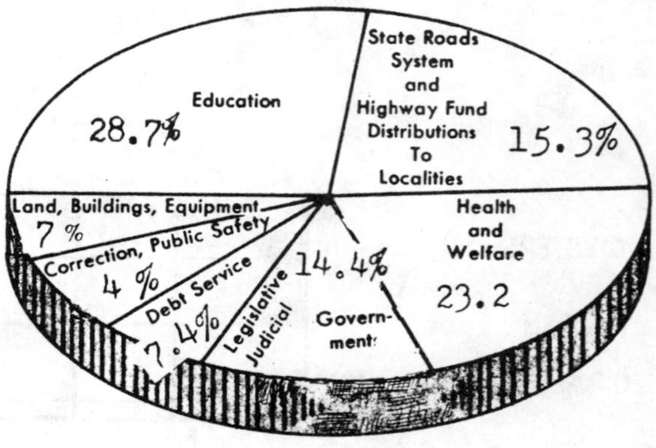

Figure F. 1979 Maryland State Spending.

United States Government

Our Federal government owns more land in Maryland than any other group or person. In our state, about 24 out of each 100 workers are busy doing some sort of state, Federal, or local government work. They earn billions of dollars a year! This is good for merchants. Why?

It all began with Maryland's gift of land for use as a national capital (1790). Many Marylanders began to work for the Federal government.

Later, more government money came into the state with the building of the ***United States Naval Academy*** at Annapolis (1845). Today, huge stretches of Maryland land are being used by several United States government agencies and by the Army, Navy, and Air Force.

Some of these large government centers are listed below, to show the kinds of work done by government employees. There are many more Federal centers. Can you name some for the class, that we have not given?

★ ★ ★

The ***National Institutes of Health*** is located in Bethesda, in Montgomery County. It has a great program of medical research. These programs may make our lives healthier, and longer! Nearby is a huge library of medical books. Across the street from the library is the ***Naval Medical Research Institute.***

In Baltimore, the U. S. Treasury Department has located the ***U.S. Coast Guard Shipyard.*** The District Office of the ***Bureau of Internal Revenue*** is in Baltimore, too. What does this office help do?

The ***Department of Agriculture*** has a huge research center at

Beltsville. On some of their land, the National Aeronautics and Space Agency has built the ***Goddard Space Flight Center.*** The Department of Agriculture has several sites in Maryland. Some are for research. Some are wildlife refuges.

Moving into a giant new building near Laurel recently, is the ***National Security Agency.*** This is very near the U. S. Army's ***Ft. George G. Meade.*** At Germantown, the ***Atomic Energy Commission*** is putting up a new headquarters on over 100 acres of Montgomery County land. At Gaithersburg, the ***National Bureau of Standards*** has moved onto 550 acres.

Andrews Air Force Base, Patuxent Naval Air Station, the ***Aberdeen Proving Grounds,*** and many, many more government agencies are located in Maryland.

DISCUSS some of the ways in which a new, big, government agency might affect a community near it. What government place is near your home? Do you know someone who works for a government? (Remember, there are city, county, state and national governments.)

SECTION XI.
EDUCATION

"There was an Old Woman,

Who lived in a shoe,

She had SO MANY CHILDREN,

She didn't know what to do!"

Can you see by the table, "Public School Enrollment" why Maryland school planners may have felt like the "Old Woman in the shoe" lately?

They ***do*** know what to do however, and are doing a very fine job.

Many schools have been built in Maryland in the past few years.

The Maryland school year does not just SEEM a little longer than in most states; it really ***is*** longer! It lasts from 180 to 185 days. You get a very good education in the time, however, because Maryland spends more on you than does the average state. In 1979-80, the average amount of money spent per pupil was nearly $2,000.

PUBLIC SCHOOL ENROLLMENT

Students

(To the nearest 10,000.)

Year	Students
1950	350,000
1960	610,000
1970	920,000
1980	810,000

Public school enrollment grew very fast after World War II ended, in 1945. Enrollment "peaked" in 1971-1972. Today enrollment is going down a little bit.

Almost half of the boys and girls who graduate from Maryland high schools go on to get more education. Many pay with student loans and scholarships.

Maryland has an excellent state-wide educational television system.

When we see how much education is in progress in our state, we can easily understand why almost one-third of the state's budget is spent on education! About ***1½ BILLION DOLLARS*** a year is spent on public education.

WHY is the education of children and young folks so important? It means first of all that the state and the nation cares a great deal about you. But, it is important for another reason, too. Much of our nation's future progress, safety and happiness depend on the students now in schools and colleges. The nation will be in your hands and depend on you when you grow up!

Maryland Educational Summary

PUBLIC SCHOOLS (FALL 1978)	
Number of schools	1,335
Enrollment (Pre-Kindergarten thru 12)	809,371
Total professional staff assigned to schools	48,303
NONPUBLIC SCHOOLS (FALL 1977)	
Number of schools	706
Enrollment (Pre-Kindergarten thru 12)	127,857
Total professional staff assigned to schools	7,819
STATE ACCREDITED COLLEGES AND UNIVERSITIES	
2 year institutions	23
Fall 1978 enrollment, full time	28,290
Fall 1978 enrollment, part time	58,804
TOTAL	87,094
4 year institutions	33
Fall 1978 undergraduate enrollment, full time	68,827
Fall 1978 undergraduate enrollment, part time	29,911
Total undergraduates	98,738
Fall 1978 graduate enrollment full and part time	26,279
Total 2 year and 4 year college enrollment	212,111

Sources: Maryland Dept. of Education; State Board of Higher Education; Washington, D.C. Board of Post-secondary Education.

Exercise.

MAKE A BAR GRAPH, PLEASE, TO SHOW HOW THE NUMBER OF STUDENTS in Maryland schools changes with the years.

Place the years (1950, etc.) at the bottom of the page. Beginning at the bottom, make 10 marks up along the left edge of your paper, an inch apart. Each of these inches will stand for 100,000 students!

A young student.

J.H.Cromwell photograph.

Exercise.

USING THE TABLE "Maryland Educational Summary," find the total number of:

(1) students going to elementary and high schools. (Include both public and private.)

(2) college students. (All.)

(3) colleges and universities. (All.)

(4) schools in Maryland. (Do not include colleges and universities.)

SECTION XII.

WINGS, RAILS, WHEELS AND WATER.

1. OUR MARYLAND HIGHWAYS

****

Freeway *a large highway with several lanes which sweeps through or around a city. A high-speed highway, usually without traffic lights. Freeways also help connect cities.*

Toll *money paid so that one can use a bridge, tunnel or highway.*

****

We are a nation on wheels! It is not unusual for a family to have two cars. Our workers travel to work on wheels. Two-thirds go to work in private automobiles; and about one-tenth use busses and trains. Nearly ***three million*** automobiles are owned by Maryland citizens. In 1979, 2,856,781 motor vehicles were registered in Maryland!

Figure 9 shows our highways, railways and airports. How are highways and railroads like veins and arteries? Could you say that they bring "life-blood" to our businesses? Not only automobiles use highways. Busses, huge trucks, taxis, all kinds of vans, use our roads.

There are trucks with special tanks to carry all sorts of liquids---gasoline, oil, milk, tar, chemicals, fertilizer! Some trucks can even keep loads refrigerated or frozen. About one of every twenty workers in our country, works in the motor vehicle industry!

All but one-fourth of our roads are paved. Most of the others are coated with gravel. Many miles of our Maryland highways are dual-lane roads.

These often have a strip of grass or trees between the lanes. What is the reason for this median strip?

Yes, the medians help prevent head-on collisions. They help shade a driver's eyes from on-coming headlights at night. Also, they look beautiful!

Freeways and Beltways. To keep cars in the business sections from being stopped by traffic, many streets are "one-way." Also, freeways are sometimes cut through larger communities.

It is now "the style" to build huge beltways around cities.

The Baltimore Beltway and the Capital Beltway (around the District of Columbia) are good examples. On a city beltway a driver circles the city as a plane circles an airport! Drivers can get into parts of the city without having to drive all the way through it. Beltways, like freeways, do not use traffic lights. These big roads help traffic move through cities more easily.

A part of the Baltimore Beltway being built a few years ago.

J. H. Cromwell photograph.

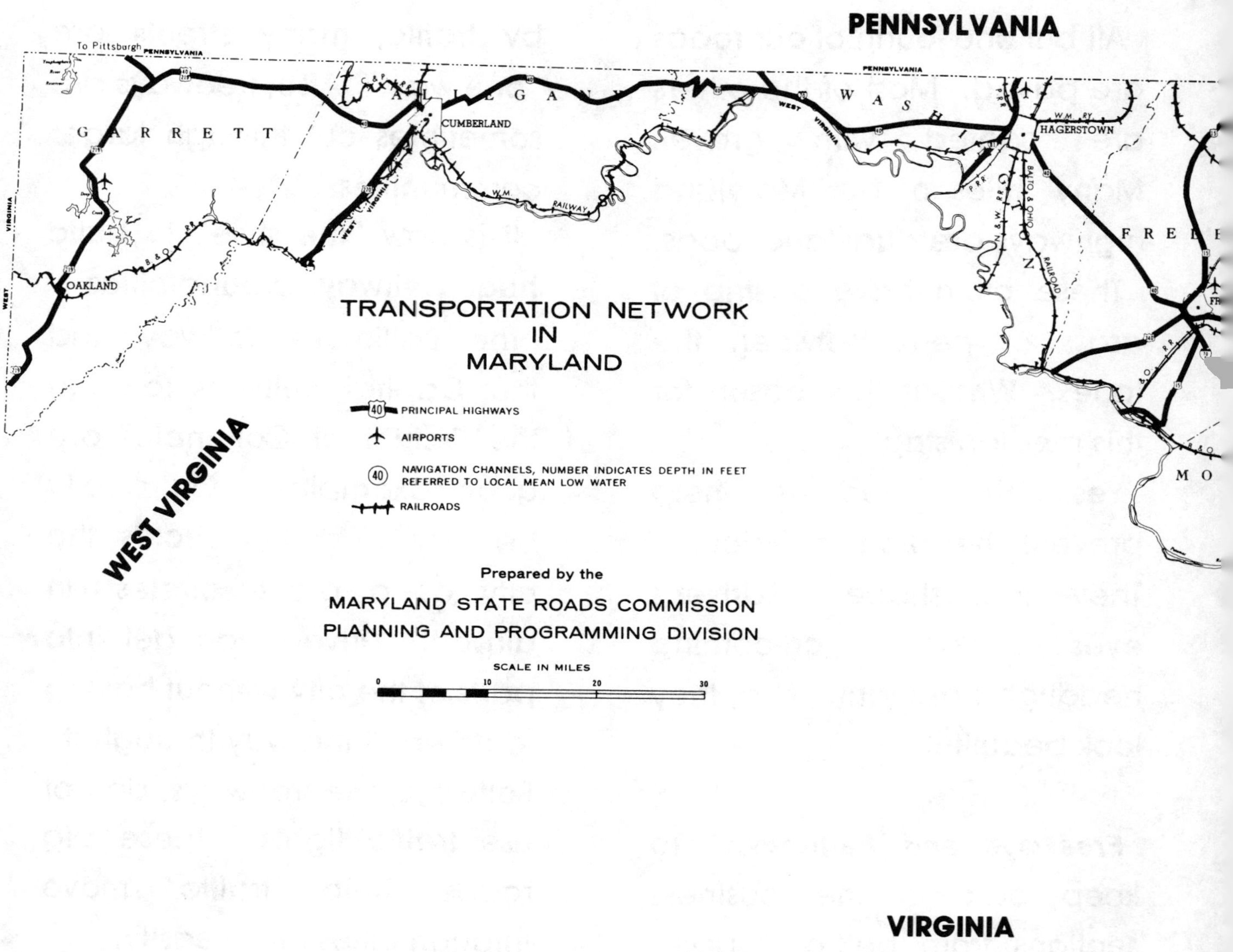

FIGURE 9. Courtesy the Maryland State Roads Commission, Planning and Programming Division.

LITHO. A. HOEN & CO., INC.

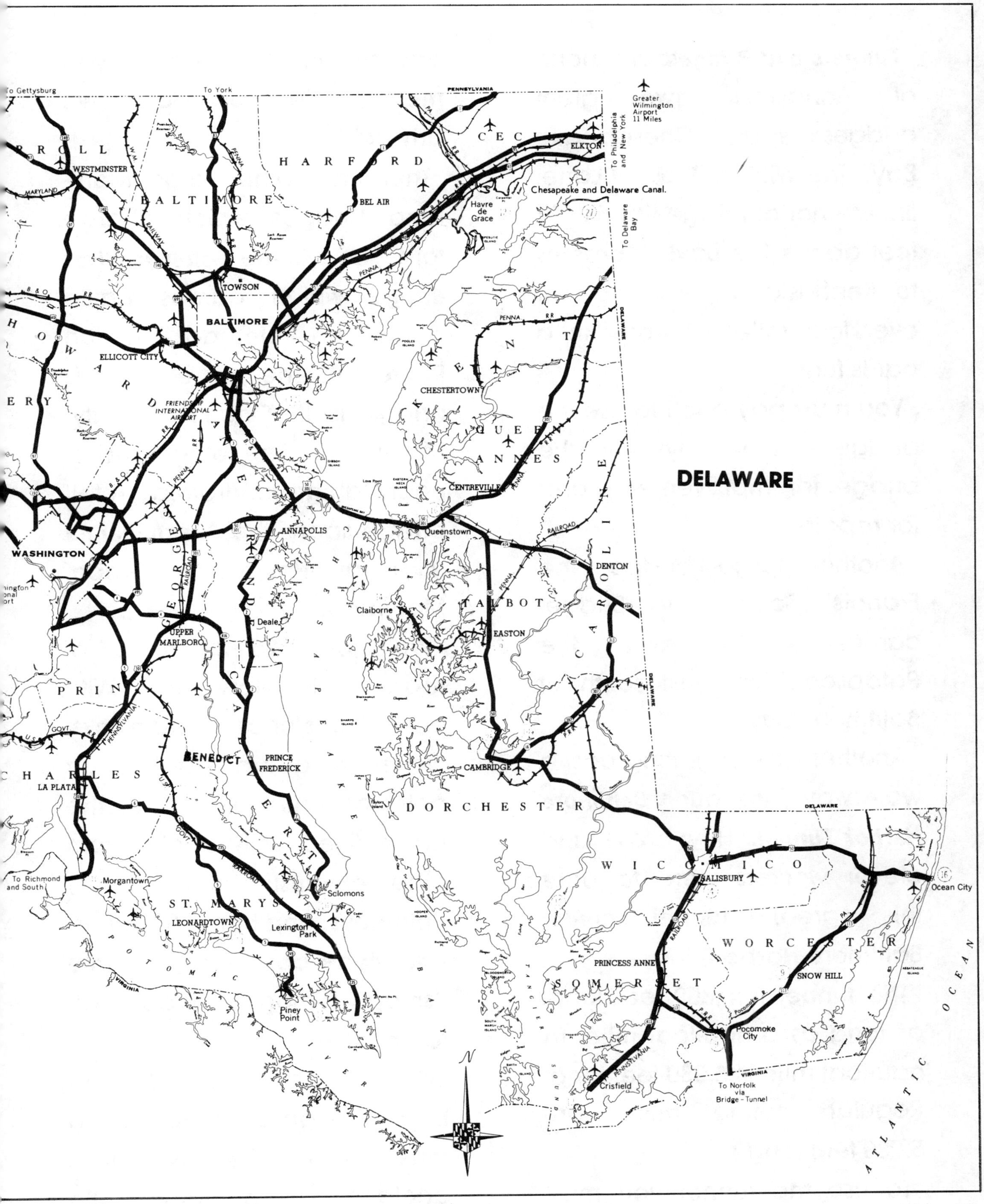
To Gettysburg
To York
PENNSYLVANIA
Greater Wilmington Airport 11 Miles
To Philadelphia and New York
CECIL
ELKTON
HARFORD
WESTMINSTER
BALTIMORE
BEL AIR
Havre de Grace
Chesapeake and Delaware Canal.
To Delaware Bay
TOWSON
BALTIMORE
HOWARD
ELLICOTT CITY
FRIENDSHIP INTERNATIONAL AIRPORT
KENT
CHESTERTOWN
QUEEN ANNES
CENTREVILLE
DELAWARE
WASHINGTON
ANNAPOLIS
Queenstown
DENTON
CAROLINE
TALBOT
Claiborne
EASTON
Deale
UPPER MARLBORO
PRINCE GEORGES
ANNE ARUNDEL
CALVERT
CHESAPEAKE BAY
BENEDICT
PRINCE FREDERICK
CAMBRIDGE
CHARLES
LA PLATA
DORCHESTER
DELAWARE
To Richmond and South
Morgantown
WICOMICO
SALISBURY
Ocean City
ST. MARYS
LEONARDTOWN
Solomons
Lexington Park
WORCESTER
PRINCESS ANNE
SOMERSET
SNOW HILL
POTOMAC RIVER
Piney Point
TANGIER SOUND
Pocomoke City
Crisfield
VIRGINIA
To Norfolk via Bridge-Tunnel
ATLANTIC OCEAN
N

Tunnels and Bridges. Just north of Annapolis, two giant bridges span Chesapeake Bay. The William Preston Lane, Jr., Memorial Bridge lifts us 187 feet above the Bay! It crosses to Kent Island. Soaring out over four miles of water in a car is fun!

You must pay a toll to use the bridge. This pays for the bridge, for improvements, and for repairs.

Another large bridge, the Francis Scott Key Bridge, carries traffic over the Patapsco River, just south of Baltimore City.

Another way of getting past a waterway is our ***Baltimore Harbor Tunnel.*** How brave and clever workers were to bore this great tunnel ***under*** Baltimore Harbor!

The tunnel is 6,300 feet long. as long as a nautical mile. (A nautical mile is 6,080 feet long. Regular statute miles are 5,280 feet long.)

To use the tunnel you must pay a toll. It can save you many miles of downtown driving.

There are other large Maryland bridges which charge tolls. One is the ***Potomac River Bridge*** which carries traffic across the Potomac River on Route 301. The east end of this bridge is in Charles County, Maryland. The other end is near Dahlgren, Virginia. A toll bridge spans the ***Susquehanna River*** at Havre de Grace, Maryland.

We have 25,823 miles of roadway in Maryland. With our millions of cars and trucks, we must guard against air pollution, "dirty air"! When the air is filled with smoke from auto exhausts, from factory chimneys, and home furnaces ---sunshine can change it into "smog." Smog is not good air to breathe!

Speaking of autos, do you know the greatest danger to girls and boys today? It is accidents, especially auto accidents! You can help prevent injury and death by remembering.

REMEMBER, it takes time to stop a car, even on dry roads. On gravel or rock roadways, it takes longer than on paved ones. Stopping is harder when the road is wet. On icy or snow-covered roads it is ***very hard*** to stop a car.

So, REMEMBER, please, to look before crossing a street. NEVER let a young child dash out into the road from behind a car or bush. Finally, REMEMBER that twilight or drizzle make seeing harder. So, be even more careful at these times. Cars are wonderful, but respect them! They are big, heavy machines.

2. RAILROADING

Do you know that Maryland had the first railroad in the country? Yes. In 1830, the Baltimore and Ohio Railroad opened a 13-mile-long railroad from Baltimore to Ellicott City. Horses pulled the cars! It was a year or so later that the first steam engine was used on "the B§O."

Today there are four large railroad companies in Maryland. They use over a thousand miles of track. Notice, on Figure 9, or on a larger map, that railroads and other roads too, seek flat land.

They go beside rivers and through mountain passes.

Railroads are working harder than ever today. We depend on them to carry gigantic amounts of freight. Even though pipe lines, trucks, and tankers have taken business from railroads, and it costs a lot to hire workers, railroads still make money on freight.

Railroads tend to lose money on passenger service. This is

not good, for people can travel, using less fuel per person, on trains. Some people commute to work on trains each day.

3. AIRPORTS

Would you like to fly to Paris? To Japan? To Florida? You can, and from one of the best jet airports in the world. Nine miles south of Baltimore is the ***Baltimore-Washington International Airport.*** It is owned by the State of Maryland. A train station is planned. It will take people from the airport into the city.

Most people do not know that the fastest-growing kind of flying is business flying in company aircraft. Thousands of small and medium-sized airplanes are owned by companies. These are often very expensive. They are used to fly executives and experts around, and to bring needed items to company plants.

Quite a few people in Maryland fly just for the fun of it. Thousands of landings each month are made at the Baltimore-Washington International Airport by small planes. Some are flying for business reasons, others for personal travel reasons.

BWI has built large air freight buildings. Tons of mail and freight travel by air today.

The four-place, Cessna ***Skylane.***

Photograph courtesy Cessna Aircraft Corp.

Planes are sometimes used by the state police. They use airplanes and helicopters to check traffic, to do planning, and to assist people in trouble.

Helicopters take people who are hurt to hospitals very quickly.

The state conservation workers use planes to help count wild animals and birds. They fly to study erosion and to do many other jobs.

There are about 40 small airports in Maryland. Some have paved runways. At other airports planes land on the grass. Almost all of these airports have people who will teach flying, give rides, or take people on trips.

Airports usually offer space to park airplanes. (Planes are flying machines, you know, so they have to be tied down firmly! If not tied down, they can fly away in strong winds!) Many small airports have workers to care for planes and to fix them. Most airports sell gasoline and oil. LOOK at Figure 9. See where the larger airports are in Maryland?

Beechcraft Super King Air, a plane often used by businesses.

Photograph courtesy Beech Aircraft.

There are large airports at Salisbury, at Easton, Hagerstown, Frederick and Cumberland. Quite a few counties have built good airports. There is a new airport at Westminster.

The biggest airport in Maryland is the ***huge*** Andrews Air Force Base near Washington, D.C. There, Air Force and Navy transports, jets, and radar planes swish in and out. The plane used by the President of the United States is kept there, too. It is called, "Air Force One."

On the Eastern Shore of Maryland much "crop dusting" is done by aircraft. Small planes or helicopters spread dust or liquids to kill insects. Seed can be planted by aircraft. Fertilizers can be spread by plane, too. Such flying is very dangerous work. Pilots must fly very close to the ground. Aerial crop treatment helps farmers to raise crops with fewer workers.

Exercise. "BRAIN-WHACKERS"!

Well for Heaven's Sake! Look! The sentences below have broken in half! Can you put them back together?

On a piece of paper, put the numbers (1) through (10). Put the letter that correctly completes the first half of the sentence by these numbers. This is not easy work. So, take your time.

(1) There are over a thousand miles of

(2)Maryland citizens own nearly

(3) Our modern highway system has

(4) To get to work

(5) The Baltimore Harbor Tunnel is

(6) Our largest *civilian* airport is

(7) Our largest *military* airport is

(8) You cross four miles of water

(9) On the Potomac River Bridge

(10) About 3/4 of all our state roads

(A) Andrews Air Force Base.

(B) Baltimore-Washington

International Airport.

(C) just about a nautical mile long.

(D) 2/3 of our workers use cars.

(E) over 25,000 miles of road.

(F) three million automobiles!

(G) railroad tracks in Maryland.

(H) tolls must be paid.

(I) are paved.

(J) traveling the Chesapeake Bay Bridge.

4. MARYLAND PORTS

Beverage *something to drink; milk, ginger ale, tea, ~~beer~~ and coffee are examples.*

Dock *deep-water space for ships by a wharf or a pier.*

Drydock *huge space from which water can be pumped to reveal ship.*

Export *to send something out of the country.*

Import *to bring things into a country from another country.*

Pier *something built out into the water, supported by poles (pilings), used to make it easier to load and unload ships.*

Wharves *piers. Places to unload or load cargo and passengers, for ships.*

Just about in the ***middle*** of Maryland, over 150 miles ***in from the ocean,*** is a huge seaport! It is the Port of Baltimore. See Figure 9. FIND the Baltimore Harbor and the Patapsco River. Can you see how ships arrive here by coming through Chesapeake Bay?

Sea captains like Baltimore's harbor. The port is further inland than most ports. This shortens the rest of the trip for their cargo. Also, cargo can be loaded directly into railway cars or onto trucks in Baltimore. These things lower costs and save time for shippers.

Another reason the Port is liked is because it has a wide, deep channel. It is 1,000 feet wide and 42 feet deep. Quite a few businessmen have asked that the channels be made 60 feet deep.

When sea captains get into the harbor at Baltimore, they have 270 piers, docks or wharves to use. There is plenty of warehouse space. There are miles of railroad track, many trucking firms and good workers at the Port. Over ***5,000 ships*** arrive in the Port each year! It is open all year long.

There is a 46-mile-long shoreline in the Port area.

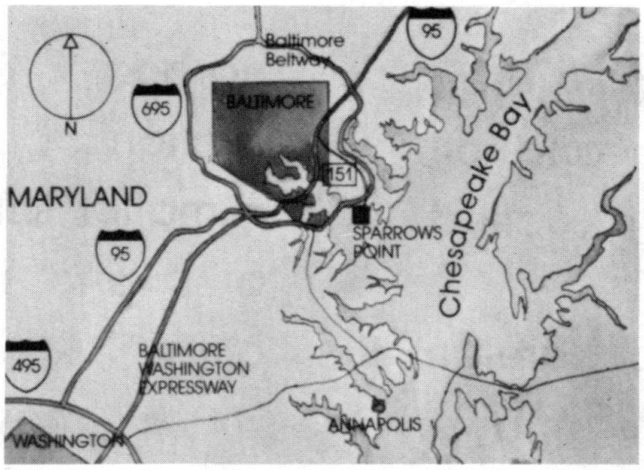

Courtesy Bethlehem Steel Corp.

About thirty miles of this has been built up with docks, piers, warehouses. (See Fig. 10). Each year, millions of tons of cargo go through the Port of Baltimore!

Many jobs depend on the port. Over 70,000 workers are needed right at the Port itself. Another 100,000 workers work with things concerned with the Port. Thanks to the Port of Baltimore, the city has become a center for steel work, copper, aluminum and chemical work. A giant sugar refinery is located at the port.

The largest waterfront business firm is Bethlehem Steel at Sparrows Point. It is one of the world's largest steel mills.

Foreign Trade. (1978 figures).

Our Port of Baltimore is the ***fifth*** greatest in the nation in foreign trade. Cargo shipped to and from other countries was worth almost 11 1/3 ***billion*** dollars in 1978. About 6 1/3 billion dollars worth of cargo was exported (shipped out). Almost 5 billion dollars worth of cargo was imported (shipped in).

When ships from other countries enter the Chesapeake Bay, they must stop and pick up a "pilot" to help them dock safely.

Coming into the Port of Baltimore, the things that were the most valuable were: machinery and transportation equipment; foreign ores; manufactured items; and oil products. These are called ***imports.***

Leaving the Port for foreign lands (***exports***) were manufactured items, machinery, automobiles, railroad equipment chemicals, oil products, grain and metals.

Shipbuilding.

Do you know that if you want to have a new ship built, or an old one fixed, that Baltimore harbor is a good place to come? Our Baltimore shipyards do about a third of all new United States shipbuilding!

There are seven giant floating drydocks, four huge shipyards and several smaller ones. There are all kinds of machinery used in shipbuilding at Baltimore, too.

The workers at the shipyards can even "stretch" a cargo ship so that it can carry more cargo. A longer middle section is built to do this.

Smaller ships and boats are built and repaired at many other Maryland shipyards. These may be found all around Chesapeake Bay. These shipyards not only have the space and machinery but they have skilled and experienced workers, as well.

Dinah Fiot drawing.

Trade Within the United States.

Going from Baltimore to other U. S. ports are steel mill products, asphalt, iron, oil and oil products, chemicals, machinery, automobiles and many other things!

Coming into Baltimore from other U.S. ports, the leading items are: oil, gasoline, phosphate rock (used for making fertilizer), and sugar.

Photograph by Joseph H. Cromwell

Other Important Waterways in Maryland.

The Port of Baltimore is the only United States port with ***two*** routes to the sea. Ships can go south by way of the Chesapeake Bay, or they can go north by the Chesapeake and Delaware Canal. LOCATE the canal on Figure 9. Ships that use the canal save 115 nautical miles. Can you see, by looking at a map of the United States, that this is true?

The Chesapeake and Delaware Canal was improved a few years ago, so that it could take more, and larger, ships. By 1970 work was done which made the canal about 450 wide and 35 feet deep.

The work also removed many of the low bridges and the bends that used to keep some large ships from using the canal. There is no toll charged for the use of the canal. Four out of ten ships that come to Baltimore use it when they leave!

There are about 70 ports in Maryland. These ship about one out of each 23 tons of freight shipped by water in the state. Seafood, wheat, sand, gravel, some metals, gasoline, oil and fertilizer are shipped from these ports. The ones on or near Chesapeake Bay include: Wicomico River, Nanticoke River, Choptank River, Tred Avon River, Chester River, Crisfield Harbor and Pocomoke River.

The Port of Cambridge can now take small ocean-going ships. The harbor there has been deepened to 25 feet.

FIND these ports in Figure 9.

The Potomac River, you may remember, belongs to Maryland for the most part. You may have seen barges, tankers and even small Navy ships going up the Potomac. Most of these are going to ports in Alexandria, Virginia and Washington, D.C.

IT'S A FACT!
A MARYLAND WATERWAY FACT !

On a sheet of paper, write the answers to the following questions:

(1) How many workers do businesses *at and near* the Port of Baltimore employ?

(2) In foreign trade, is the Port of Baltimore 3rd, 4th, or 5th greatest in the nation?

(3) How many nautical miles can ships save, when they want to go north from Baltimore, by using the Chesapeake and Delaware Canal?

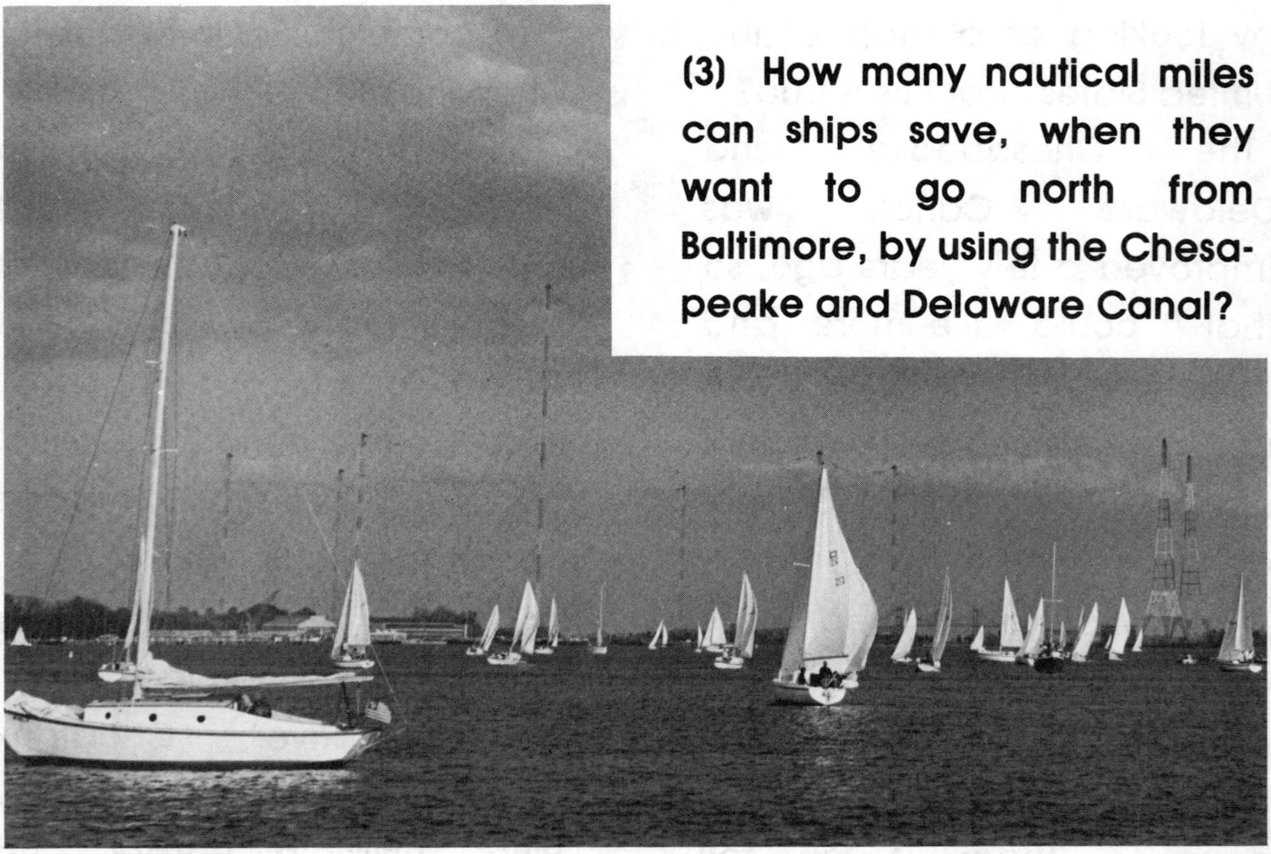

Sailboats on the Severn River, Annapolis, Maryland.

J. H. Cromwell photograph.

SECTION XIII.

BALTIMORE CITY

Baltimore City as seen from the air. Note Charles Center, the inner harbor area and the Civic Center.

J. H. Cromwell photograph.

★★★

Blight *a withering away; not prosperous; does not grow.*
Lagoon *shallow lake or pond near the sea.*
Retail *selling in small quantities or packages directly to the public.*
Wholesale *selling in large quantities to stores or salesmen.*

★★★

Baltimore City began in 1729 on sixty lots bought from Charles and Daniel Carroll. By 1850 Baltimore had grown so much and had so many people, it was made a "separate political unit" the following year.

This means that Baltimore City is not a part of any county. Baltimore is one of three cities in the United States which have their own government, with no county government above them.

Since 1851, of course, Baltimore has grown, and grown and GROWN! She has overflowed her city lines. She is surrounded by land covered with houses and businesses. Inside the city lines, however, as you can see by the map (Figure 10), Baltimore has 79 square miles of land area and 7 square miles of water area.

Is this water area wasted? Not at all! The Port of Baltimore has a traffic of over ***11 billion*** dollars a year! Just think, too, 70,000 people work at the port. Experts say about another 100,000 work in the city for companies that use the Port.

There are four large parks and many smaller parks in the city. Baltimore has many monuments, statues and parks. The first monument built to honor George Washington stands in Mt. Vernon Place.

You can see there, also, statues of other famous men. Fort McHenry is another famous Baltimore City place. Do you know its story? Our national flag flies there 24 hours a day.

At Pratt and Albemarle Streets you can visit a museum called the Flag House. There are several fine museums in Baltimore.

There are so many interesting places, full of history, in Baltimore that we do not have space to mention them all.

To mention just two places---The Shot Tower---is a most unusual building. It is 234 feet high and was built in 1829. Do you know what it was used for?

The oldest house in the city still standing is Mount Clare. It was the home of Charles Carroll, the Barrister. He was a rich man and a patriot of the new United States during the Revolutionary War. The city owns his home now.

Washington Monument, Baltimore.

J. H. Cromwell photograph.

Can you see the Baltimore Beltway on the map in Figure 10? This highway helps cut down traffic in the center of Baltimore City. Baltimore was planned over 200 years ago, so the city streets are rather narrow. New expressways were built to move traffic quickly around and through the city.

TELL ME, PLEASE:

Exercise

How old is Baltimore City?

What is the *total* area of the city?

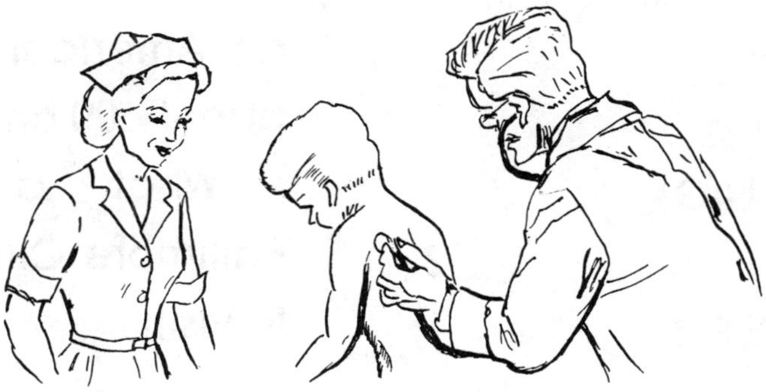

People come from all over the world to be treated in Baltimore hospitals. Johns Hopkins Hospital and Medical School is the largest of these. It has 1,097 beds (1978 count). Thousands of bed-patients, out-patients and emergency cases are helped by over 5,150 hospital workers.

The next largest hospital is the University Hospital. In 1978 it had 680 beds ready for use. At University Hospital over 2,400 workers keep busy with many cases. There are eleven other large hospitals in the Baltimore Metropolitan area. These hospitals care for thousands of patients every year. You can see why people come from all over the world to Baltimore, to get the best of medical care.

There are two ***important*** things that hospitals do, in addition to helping those who are sick or hurt. Can you unscramble the following words to find what these are? Hospitals find these two things very important. Write the "un-scrambled" words on a sheet of paper, please.

(1) R A I N T I N G

(2) A R C H S E E R

Education Center in Many Ways

Free to all, are art galleries, museums, parks and libraries in Baltimore City. The Baltimore Symphony Orchestra is one of the first founded by an American city. There are about 600 churches in the city.

What a grand place Baltimore City is to live in and to visit!

Exercise.

SEE FIGURE 10. SEE THE AREA INSIDE THE BALTIMORE CITY LIMITS.

LOCATE THE BALTIMORE BELTWAY.

SEE THE LAND AREA AROUND BALTIMORE CITY.

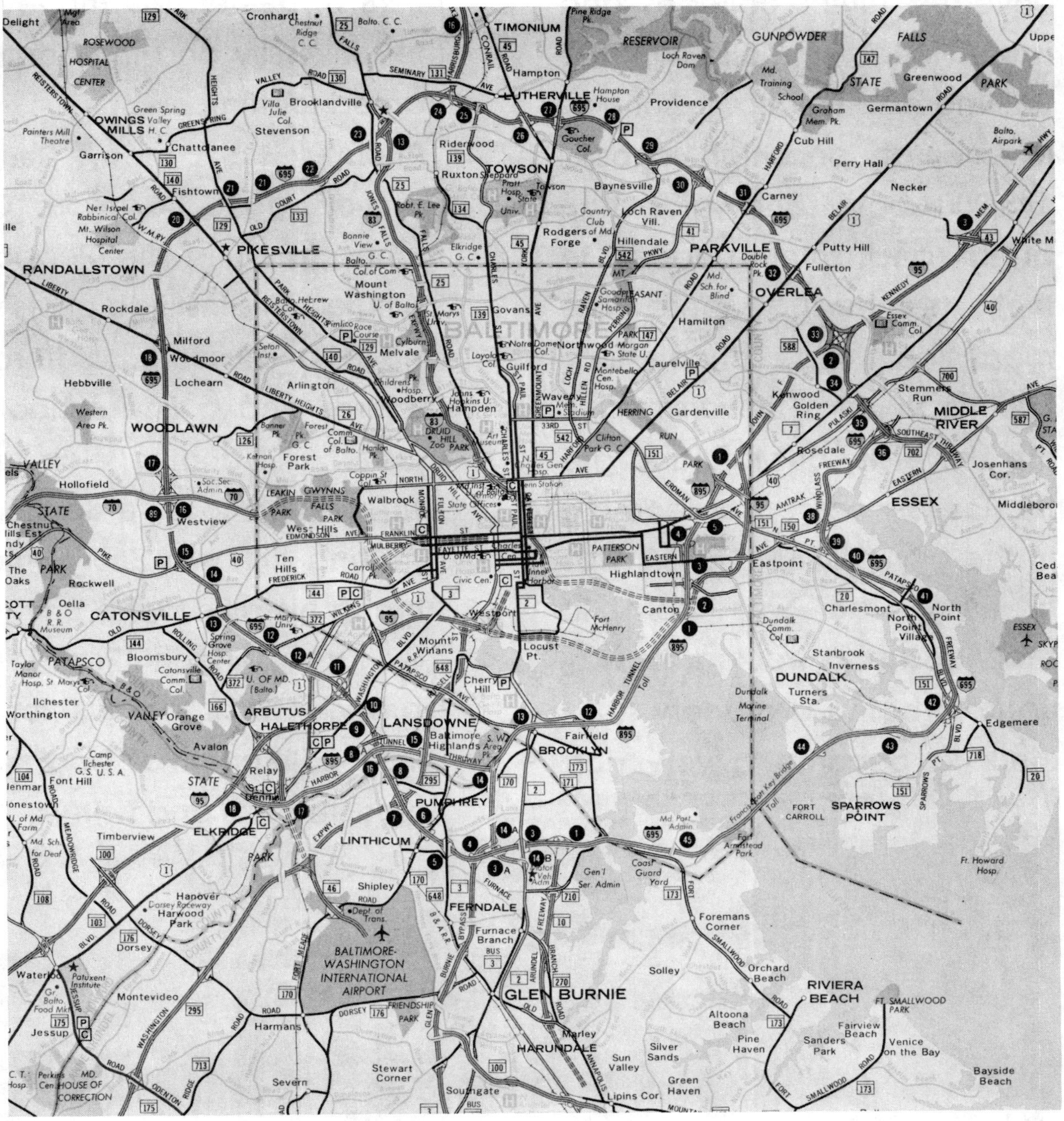

Figure 10. Baltimore City and Vicinity.

Courtesy the State Roads Commission of Maryland, Planning and Programming Division.

In Baltimore, in addition to all the teaching going on in the hospitals, there are twenty colleges, junior colleges and professional schools! In the Baltimore public schools (elementary and high schools) 145,500 boys and girls turn bright and shining faces to their teachers! There are many fine private schools, too.

Johns Hopkins University and the University of Maryland are the largest centers of learning in the city. ***Johns Hopkins*** was a man who was born in Maryland and worked his way up from being a grocery store clerk to become a very rich businessman. He was quite powerful in railroad and bank management. When he died in 1873, he left his money to the university and the hospital named for him.

Another rich man, ***George Peabody,*** gave Baltimore City money to build the Peabody Institute. This institute offers the public a museum, a library, lectures and a fine school of music. Still another rich man who wanted to give Baltimore a lasting gift, was ***Enoch Pratt.*** Among his gifts to the city was the large Enoch Pratt Free Library. It is famous for its large collection of books. It helps students and writers.

The Baltimore Museum of Art. J. H. Cromwell photograph.

How's Business?

If some one were able to ask the city of Baltimore how business was, she could say, "Oh, not bad. A few billion here, and a few billion there!" It's true. There are over 5,000 retail stores in the city. They sell things worth over two ***billion*** dollars a year!

Most of Baltimore City's ***retail stores*** are downtown or in her 25 shopping centers. Many of these shopping centers offer free parking. They group many kinds of stores and businesses together. Outside the city, many other firms make things and sell things. Businesses find it a good idea to be near the Baltimore Beltway, or another big road. Why is this?

Outside Baltimore in the counties that surround the city, new homes, schools and shopping centers are built every year. There are now about 165 shopping centers just outside Baltimore City.

Baltimore City has a ***wholesale trade*** of almost four ***billion*** dollars a year! Can you see how the ***location*** of the city, her good roads, railways, seaport and airport help business?

There are about 1,100 manufacturing plants in Baltimore City. Many are the largest of their kind in the nation. About 670 of the manufacturers, however are small---with less than 20 workers.

Baltimore manufacturers make all sorts of things! Steel

The *USS Constellation* in Baltimore's Inner Harbor. J. H. Cromwell photograph.

is made in Baltimore, spices are packaged, meat is canned. Some plants make telephone and electrical equipment. Others assemble cars and trucks. Baltimore manufacturers make venetian blinds, weather instruments, missiles, nuclear equipment, bottle caps, enamel, radar and radios, X-ray machinery and straw hats! Some manufacturers process chemicals.

Baltimore is an interesting place to work. Plants in the city make over seven ***billion*** dollars worth of things each year. That is, they "add value" dollars by their work. With so many different things to make and to do, Baltimore City seldom feels a business "slump."

The city government is, of course, located in Baltimore. Also, many important offices of the State of Maryland are in the city. The Maryland State Department of Education, the State Roads Commission and many others have headquarters in Baltimore City.

The oldest house in Baltimore City, the Mount Clare Mansion.

J. H. Cromwell photograph.

Courtesy the Maryland State Roads Commission, Planning and Programming Division.

What Now?

"City blight" has hurt the center of many large cities. In Baltimore, planners are working hard to keep the city's downtown section healthy.

Slow traffic, tottering old buildings and a lack of parking can "strangle" a city. To prevent this, Baltimore rebuilt a 33-acre part of the business section. It is now called Charles Center. There you can find offices, places to eat and live, meeting places, a theater and many parking spaces!

There was a plan, too, for the inner part of Baltimore harbor. The city has built a lagoon there. Pleasure boats sail past. By the water is a beautiful park. Here people can rest, stroll, visit shops nearby. They can find nice places to eat. Or they can stop to watch boats move across the water.

A second Baltimore Beltway around the city is planned. Yes, Baltimore City is a town with much history, but one that is ***not*** standing still!

Columbia, Maryland
Employment / 26,000 Jobs

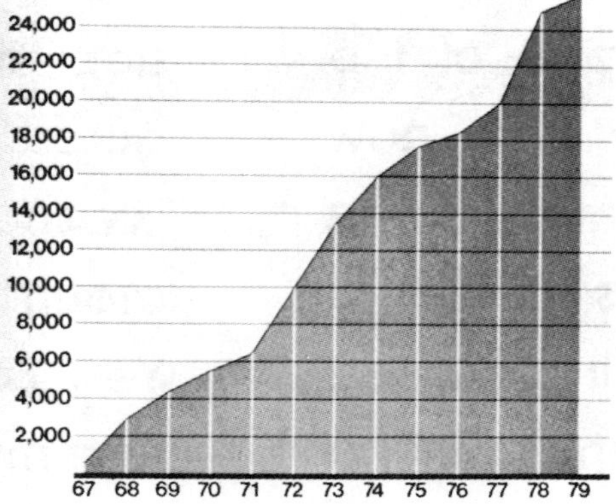

SECTION XIV.
MUSHROOM CITIES

★★★

Leisure *a person's spare time.*
"Mini-bus" *a small bus.*
Retired *an older person who leaves full-time work is "retired".*
Townhouses *several homes built in a row with no space between them. Most have a small garden. Often they have an upstairs, a main floor, and a lower level.*

★★★

Something new and important is happening. In our state whole towns are "mushrooming" up! Eleven are presently being built.

Some towns are like mushrooms. One day you see only bare fields and trees; then, several months later, you look and see a whole community! Mushrooms grow like that. They suddenly pop up from the ground.

Cities used to spread slowly. They would swallow up smaller towns as they grew. One by one, houses and apartments were built. A mile or so at a time, water mains, power lines and gas mains were laid as the city grew. Today, as you learned when you studied the population facts, more and more people are coming to live near Baltimore and near Washington, D.C. So, our cities are growing ***very fast.***

Builders today can build homes much faster than they could a few years ago. They have learned to use parts of houses which have been put together in factories. This is called ***prefabrication.*** Also, builders can now use great earth moving machines, graders, bulldozers, to shape the building places. Cement can now be poured very fast.

Now think a moment. What will this mean? If a large community is suddenly built in a county, what will it mean to businessmen there? Will school planners need to think about this new town?

And, before he builds, won't the person who wants to develop and sell the land have to think of many things? He or she needs to know if there will be people ready to buy the homes. How to get water, sewers, gas and electricity to the site must be considered.

County workers need to think about improving roads when new people come. Also, plans must be made for shops, churches, recreation areas.

Are these planned towns a good thing? Are they better than the slow sprawl of a city which grows without much planning? We don't like to see row after row of houses which are all alike. But, can a builder make a profit if many different styles of homes are built?

There is a lot of "Yes," and a

lot of "No," and quite a few 'Maybes," in planning towns. New people bring new business, but they need services from the county, too. Land values will rise near the new town, but taxes may rise too! Also, all these new people will be voting and may change the local governments. DISCUSS these "mushroom cities" in your class, please.

Our "Old" New City!

In 1936 only woods and fields were to be seen where the city of Greenbelt is today. A new idea for a town was being talked about in Washington, D. C. Housing was badly needed for the men and women who worked for the government and who were in the military services.

Planners in Washington wanted to try building a new kind of city, an ***experimental*** town. At first Greenbelt was owned by the United States government. The goverment experts wanted to build homes that people could afford. They also wanted to make jobs for people out of work.

Instead of just building row after row of houses, the planners of Greenbelt said, "Let's plan a whole town." Why not put in the center of the town a shopping place with a theater?" A town meeting hall, a library, a swimming pool could be there, too.

Another new idea was to make walkways go under roads so that people could safely walk through the town. The children could walk to school more safely. Places were chosen for churches, schools and parks. In 1937 building began in Prince George's County, Maryland.

Once Greenbelt was built and filled with people, city planners from all over the world came to see it. They looked at the handy town shopping center. They saw the paved plaza where people could sit and visit. They looked at the big steam plants that piped steam heat to houses and apartments from central locations. They went away and used many of the new things they had seen.

Today over 12,000 people live in Greenbelt. The city is still growing.

New Ideas in Building---

Shopping Centers

After World War II ended in 1945, Americans turned back to peacetime work. Many young people married and had children. Many homes were needed. Builders were busy.

And---a very important fact---thousands of automobiles began pouring off factory assembly lines again! Traffic, traffic! If you wanted to drive downtown to buy something, it was a long trip and a slow one. Soon, too, it was very hard to find a place to park.

The idea, used in Greenbelt, of communities with stores, services, theaters, all grouped in the center with plenty of parking there, was a good one.

Builders began to copy this plan. They grouped drug stores, grocery stores, hardware stores and filling stations in shopping centers.

Department store managers saw all these people living in the suburbs, too. They decided to build stores on the edges of cities.

So, the idea of grouping all these businesses together with plenty of free parking nearby made good sense. The idea worked. The new shopping centers were very successful.

A shopping center, opened in 1981, Greenbelt, Md.

Author's photograph.

As you might guess, this was good for people in the suburbs but bad for stores in the middle of large cities. People went to suburban shopping centers and did not drive downtown. Soon, center city business managers asked that subway lines be built. They decided to build parking garages.

Two things were important. The many new homes outside cities and the many, many automobiles now in use!

A Maryland Mushroom City---Belair in Bowie

In Prince George's County, a company bought a large estate called "Belair." The company kept the name for their new development.

The beautiful old mansion and a double line of ancient tulip poplar trees were left unharmed. This red brick home was built in the early 1700s for a governor of Maryland. Horse racing in the United States is said to have started here.

Work began on Belair in 1960. The community became a part of the town of Bowie nearby. The votes of the people who came to live in Belair changed the government of Bowie.

Today, 42,000 people live in the Belair development.

There are eight elementary schools, two junior high schools, a parochial school and a large senior high school. In the shopping centers are many stores with plenty of parking near them.

Three community swimming pools and several tennis courts have been made.There is a good bicycle trail.

Many churches have been built. There are about half a dozen home designs. Some are small, some are large.

On the eleven square miles of land, there are about 10,000 homes. More homes are under construction.

A Mushroom City---
Leisure World

Some new towns are being built for older people only. You see, retired people like certain things in their homes. They may not want to have to climb stairs. They may no longer feel like taking care of lawns and large houses.

In the summer of 1966 in Montgomery County, people began to move into a new community. It is called Rossmoor Leisure World. To live there you must be at least 50 years old. It is being built on 600 acres. Thousands of living units are planned. Over 2800 families live there now.

In the Rossmoor town the retired people may use a clubhouse, a swimming pool, a golf course. They live in several kinds of apartments and houses. The town is fenced and guarded to make it a very safe place.

Washington, D. C. is near Rossmoor. It is easy to get there for shopping, museums, theaters and sightseeing. Several other large Maryland towns are near.

Another Example of Planned Building

In Anne Arundel County a new city has been built around a beautiful golf course. This city is for both young and old people. Its name is Crofton.

There is a club there for parties and meetings. There is the big golf course and clubhouse. There is a huge swimming pool. By Crofton is a 27-acre shopping center.

Over one-fourth of the land in Crofton is to be kept in grass, trees, ponds and gardens. It is near Annapolis, Washington, D. C., and Baltimore. Over 2500 families live there now. When it is complete the city will have 3500 homes.

Newest and Largest Mushroom City of Them All!

HUGE is the word for the town being built in Howard County. It is named Columbia. NEW is another good word for Columbia---new ideas!

Land was bought by a large company---14,000 acres! Then company managers talked with county and state planning people. New zoning was approved for Columbia. Work began in the summer of 1966. By 1980, about 53,000 people had moved into homes in Columbia.

What makes people happy in a city? Mr. James Rouse of Baltimore, head of the company which was to build Columbia, wanted to know. He called together experts on education, on people, on business---and asked them this question.

The experts said that people are happiest in rather small

neighborhoods, which are in a medium-sized town, near a large town. So, Mr. Rouse and his planners decided to build nine "villages" with three to four neighborhoods in each. These villages will surround the center of the city.

In the center of Columbia are apartment houses, businesses, office buildings, a huge shopping mall, a library, theaters, meeting places, churches, a hospital, stores and many other things! There is a large artificial lake, too.

If you live in Columbia and want something not sold by the village shopping center, you may take a mini-bus to the center of the city. (These little busses have their own roadways.) Also, for other things, people can easily go to Baltimore and Washington, D. C.

Children may walk to village schools safely. Auto traffic is carefully planned. Schools are medium in size, so that students will not feel lonely.

In Columbia homes are built in many styles. There are several small lakes and a golf course. Some homes are small for those with small incomes. Others are larger, and can be bought by those who have earned their way up to larger salaries!

Over 100,000 people will one day live in Columbia, Mr. Rouse estimates. It is thought that about half the people living there will also work there. Jobs will be available for many workers. Plants which pay good salaries, do work that is not noisy, that does not make smoke and fumes, are to be built into the city. Columbia City leaders hope to attract "clean industry." Firms that do research would be an example of such work places. Can you think of others?

The ideas we have talked about and many more will go

into making this new city of Columbia. How will it work out? Will this new Maryland city be a model for other new cities all over the world? We will know in a few more years!

Yes, in Maryland today there is a new kind of town building. Whole cities are being built from ***plans.*** They are being built ***much faster*** than ever before. In the homes are air conditioners, dishwashers, and all sorts of ***equipment*** that we would not have found in an ordinary house just a few years ago.

ACTIVITY

(a) Draw a plan for a small community. Give it a shopping center. Name the kinds of stores you think that people will need. Don't forget, the stores must have enough business to make a profit.

(B) Draw a plan for a new city. What a lot of things it will need! Don't forget the schools now! You may find that you will need several boys and girls to work on this plan.

Make a list of the things you will have to think about, before you draw out your city plan.

SECTION XV. ENERGY IN MARYLAND

Energy definitions !

Air pollution	*air with smoke, dust, gases and chemicals in it; dirty air.*
Conservation	*to save; to conserve; not waste.*
Energy	*power to make things move; people eat food for energy; machines must have a fuel to give them energy to work, to move.*
Fuel	*something taken in to give energy. Food is our fuel; cars use gasoline. Coal and wood are fuels.*
Nuclear energy	*energy made by splitting atoms! A controlled chain reaction in a nuclear power plant makes nuclear energy.*
Nuclear reactor	*a machine that uses the metal uranium (usually) to make energy, nuclear energy.*
Nuclear wastes	*metal rods, liquids, other things which have taken in radiation and must be put in a safe place. They can send out rays (radiation) and can be a health problem.*
Petroleum	*an oily liquid which will burn; oil.*
Radiate	*to go out through air or space; metal "radiates" its heat, you can feel this heat without touching the metal. Heat and light radiate from the sun, for example.*
Radiation	*rays sent out, traveling and being received.*
Solar power	*is energy in the form of heat and light that comes from the sun.*

1. WHAT IS ENERGY?

Energy makes things go. Everything that moves, that works, that goes---needs some kind of ***energy.***

It takes energy to make people and animals live and move. Energy is needed to cause automobiles, trains and airplanes to go. We need energy to keep our houses and schools warm in the winter, cool in the summer!

Can you think of other everyday things that use energy?

To get energy we must use a ***fuel.*** Food is our fuel. Food is changed into energy in our bodies. Animals eat to get their energy, too. So, ***food is a fuel.***

Oil is a fuel. No, we certainly must ***not*** eat oil! But most cars and aircraft today use a fuel called gasoline. Some cars, trains, trucks, tractors and busses use a fuel called diesel oil. Both gasoline and diesel oil is made from oil. Oil is often called ***petroleum.*** It is pumped from wells drilled into the ground.

Electricity is power, energy, a sort of fuel. As you know, electricty makes many things in our homes work---our electric lights, stoves, ovens, clothes dryers and television sets.

Can you think of other things in your home that are run on electricity?

Trains often use electrical power. There are several kinds of electric cars and trucks. In November, 1980, the first airplane to use electrical power from solar cells, flew!

Natural gas is a fuel. Natural gas is found by drilling wells. Now remember, we don't mean gasoline, we are talking right now about natural gas, a vapor that will burn.

Uses of Energy in Maryland (1973).
(In Percentages of Total BTUs)

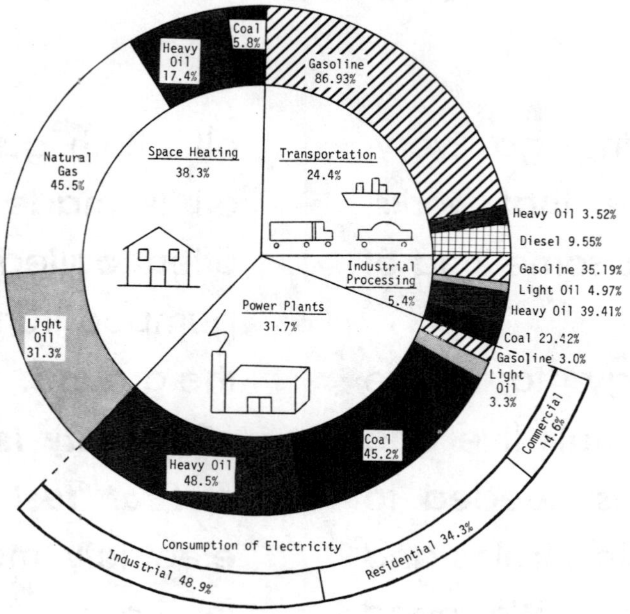

Source: Based on data from the Maryland Air Quality Control Agency and Federal Power Commission Statistics.

Tanker and barge movements bringing oil into Maryland.

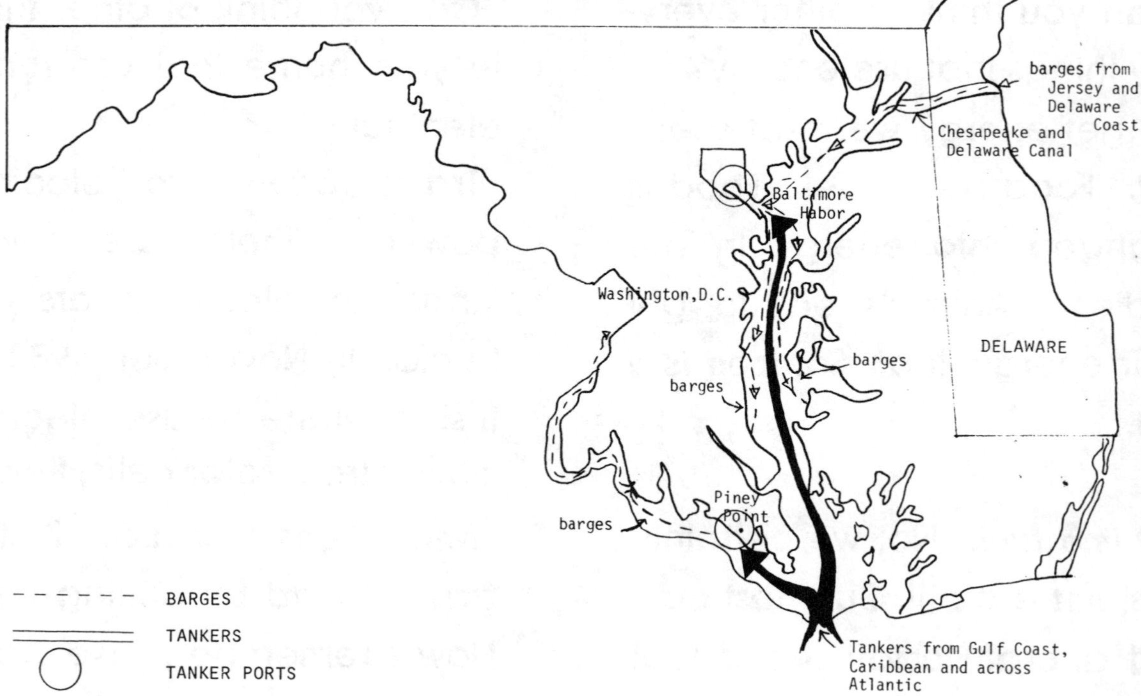

Above illustrations courtesy the State of Maryland, Energy Policy Office. From *Profile of the Maryland Petroleum Industry.*

Manufactured gas is another form of gas, a vapor, that will burn. It is made by combining certain chemicals and other things. Both natural and manufactured gas can be used to heat homes, to use in air conditioners, for stoves and clothes dryers.

Solar energy is a fuel. We can use the heat from the sun to heat homes and other buildings. Also, sunlight can make electrical power when it shines on "solar cells."

2. ENERGY USES

Heating and Cooling.

Almost all homes now have ***central heating.*** That is, a furnace to make the heat in one place. This heat is then sent to the rooms of the house. We use a great deal of fuel to heat our homes each year. What fuels do we use to heat homes?

Before 1950, few of our homes had air conditioning. Just a few places of business were air conditioned. Yes, it was very hot at times. Schools were not cooled. People just ***wilted*** when the temperatures were high.

Today, we use huge amounts of energy to cool our homes, schools, work places, stores and homes.

Transportation Energy Use.

We use a great deal of fuel (energy) in transportation. Our automobiles use gasoline, diesel oil and some alcohol. Trucks use gasoline and diesel oil. Aircraft and trains also need fuel.

The ships we see at the Port of Baltimore and on Maryland waterways, they use fuel.

Also, in recent years we have used quite a bit of energy to air condition cars, trains, planes and busses.

In transportation we mostly use oil and oil products!

Gasoline Used in Maryland.

In 1972, Marylanders used about 1.8 ***billion*** gallons of gasoline. In 1978, we used over 2 ***billion*** gallons!

As you might guess, about 95 per cent of the gasoline used in Maryland is for higway use. A small amount is used by tractors, boats and aircraft.

Chevrolet Caprice Classic

EXERCISE

1. List ways that energy is used in an office building.
2. How is energy used in a department store?
3. In a grocery store, how is energy used?
4. How does your school use energy?
5. In your home, how is energy used?
6. What kinds of fuel are used in transportation by trains, busses, ships and aircraft?
7. What is the difference between natural gas and gasoline?
8. What fuel do people need for energy?
9. Name two kinds of fuel that automobiles can use.
10. Where does petroleum come from? Is it made from trees? Is it found in the ground?

You can find more information on energy in books and magazines

3. ELECTRICAL ENERGY IN MARYLAND

Fuel Consumed by the Maryland Electric Utility Industry

Coal	**1970**	**1974**	**1979**
Total consumption tons	12,091,486	10,042,269	12,025,829
Total cost	$140,855,741	$228,221,422	$407,637,164
Average price per ton*	$10.81	$21.09	$33.32

Burning one ton of coal produces about the same amount of energy as burning 4 barrels of oil.

Oil (includes all oil types)	**1970**	**1974**	**1979**
Total consumption in barrels	16,565,387	38,938,814	22,920,171
Total cost	$43,539,975	$435,651,572	$420,053,861
Average price per barrel	$2.63	$11.18	$18.33

Courtesy, Maryland Electric Utility Council

In Maryland, electrical power is made at great power plants.

This illustration shows what kinds of fuels are used to make our electricity in Maryland. As you can see, coal, oil and nuclear energy are our three big ways of making electricity.

The word "hydro" in the graph, means that this electricity was made by using the energy of water. You can use the force of water falling over a waterfall or over a dam to turn a turbine. The ***turbine*** is a machine that makes electricity.

When oil, coal or nuclear energy is used in making electricity---they are used to heat water until it turns into steam. The steam then pushes powerfully and turns a turbine.

In Maryland the sale of electricity has ***just about doubled*** in the past ten years. We are using more and more power!

There are 21 power plants in Maryland. They can generate 8,547 MW of power!

Who owns these power companies? Most are owned by the people and groups buying stocks and bonds in the company. Some power companies, however, are owned by cooperatives. (Groups of people who all own a share in the company. They then use the power themselves.) Some power companies are owned by towns or cities.

Retail Sales of Electricity in Maryland by Type of Electric Utility System

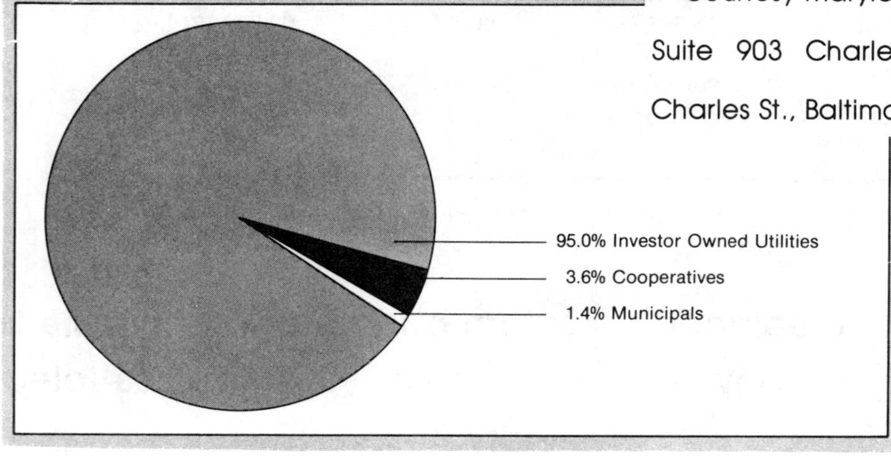

Courtesy Maryland Electric Utility Council, Suite 903 Charles Center, South, 36 S. Charles St., Baltimore, Maryland 21201.

4. COAL IN MARYLAND.

Quite a bit of coal is mined in Western Maryland. Much of this is shipped out of the state. A great deal of the coal we burn in our power plants and factories comes from other states.

Nearly 11 ***million*** tons of coal went through the Port of Baltimore in the year 1977. The Port is the nation's ***second largest coal export*** port! It may be ***the*** largest in the U. S. if more coal loading places are built. Also, channels need to be deepened to allow bigger ships to reach the coal docks.

5. Petroleum

Movements

Oil and other petroleum products (things made from oil) make up a large part of the Port of Baltimore's trade.

We can't say that this is all used in Maryland. Much of it goes on to other places in the United States. The large amounts going through the Port of Baltimore, however, tell us how important oil is to Maryland and the other states.

For example: 1.8 million TONS of gasoline came through the Port in 1977. Plus over 2 million TONS of distillate fuel oil, and 1/2 a million TONS of crude (not refined) petroleum.

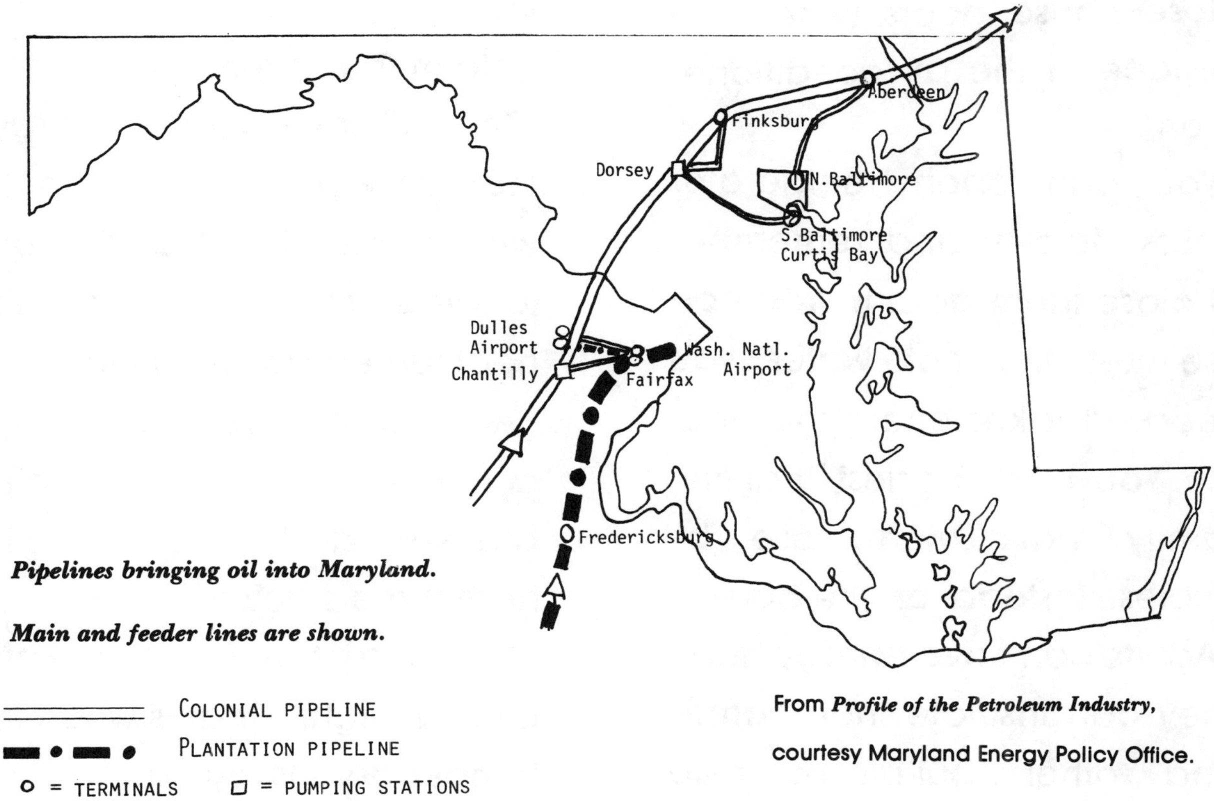

Pipelines bringing oil into Maryland.

Main and feeder lines are shown.

From ***Profile of the Petroleum Industry,*** courtesy Maryland Energy Policy Office.

6. SAVING OUR ENERGY

We can all help save energy. We want to do this because we want to make our world oil last as long as possible. One day, the oil will run out. Before then we must find new ways to get the energy we need.

What can you do to save energy? You can turn off lights, radios, and television sets that are not needed. A great saving of energy is made when you remember to close house doors (when the furnace or the air conditioner is on).

You can open refrigerator doors quickly and remember to close them again. You can use just the hot water you need. It takes energy to heat it. You can suggest that the family walk more, use bicycles, instead of the car!

Adults can save energy, too. They can insulate their homes and other buildings, add storm windows and doors.

In the winter, the family can curtain windows that face northward (away from the sun). At night, these curtains can be shut. When cold winds blow from the north, curtains can be pulled shut. On the sunny side of the house, the curtains should be opened to let in sunshine.

We can all set our ***thermostats*** to save energy. We can set them so that the house is not too hot in the winter, nor too cold in the summer!

This will save a lot of energy. We can wear a sweater in the winter. This will let us be comfortable yet let us keep the heat turned down a little.

At night we can use comforters and electric blankets and sleep with the heat turned down.

You see, the furnace works most at night. That is when the temperature is lowest.

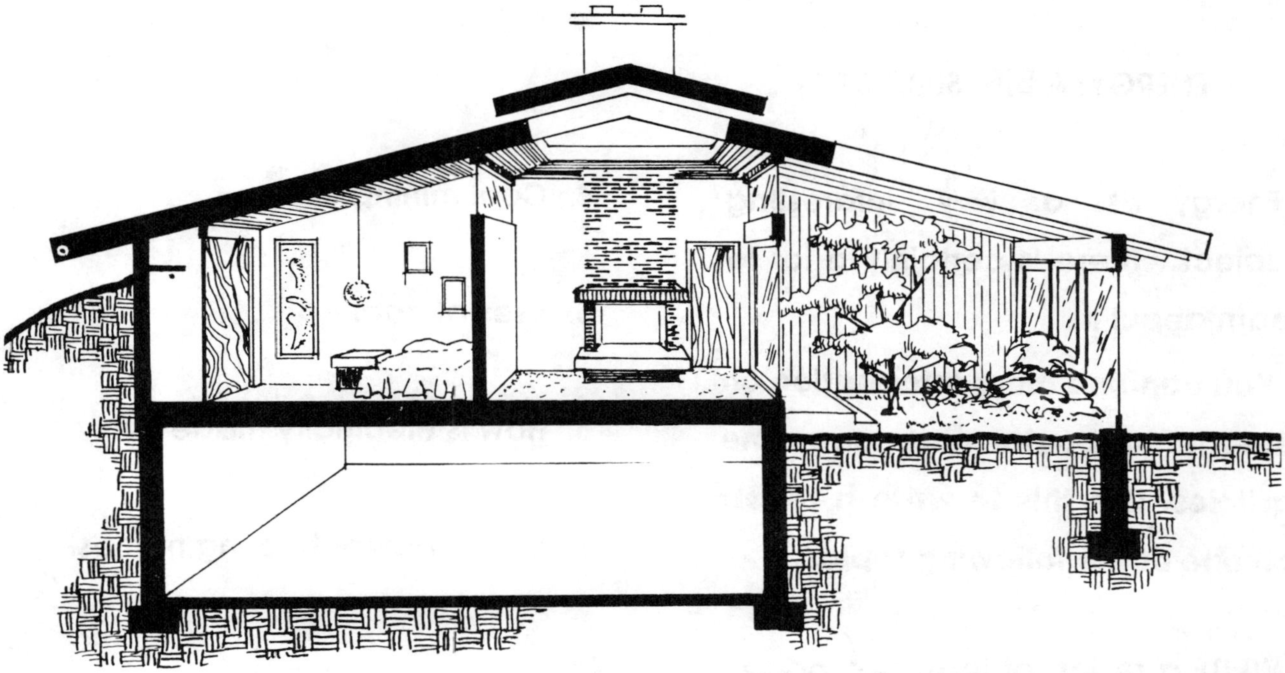

Section:
Energy Conscious House

An Energy counscious house!

Perspective:
Energy Conscious House

From ***Passive Design,*** U.S.Dept. of Energy.

EXERCISE

ENERGY: A BIG SUBJECT.

Energy is a *very* interesting subject. There is certainly a lot to learn about it!

You can find more information on energy in books and magazine articles. Use this to write a report on one of the following topics.

WRITE a report at least two pages long. Choose one of the ideas below. **READ your report to your class.**

If you read the reports, *your class* will know a great deal about energy!

SUBJECT

1. Oil. What is it? How is it gotten out of the ground?

2. Uses of oil in Maryland.

3. Problems of oil use. (Lack of oil. Air pollution.)

4. Coal mining.

5. Uses of coal.

6. How is electricity made?

7. Solar heat for heating homes.

8. Using solar power to make electricity.

9. Electric cars and trucks.

10. Nuclear energy---what are its uses?

11. Nuclear power --- problems.

12. Water power. (Hydro power.)

13. Geothermal energy.

14. Natural gas. How is it gotten from the earth?

15. Cars and fork lifts that use propane gas. (Not gasoline.)

16. Wind energy for electrical power and for pumps.

17. Wind energy for transportation. (Water transport.)

18. Future energy from satellite power stations. (A National Aeronautics and Space Administration project.)

19. Geothermal energy from the earth and volcanoes.

20. Seawater power plants!

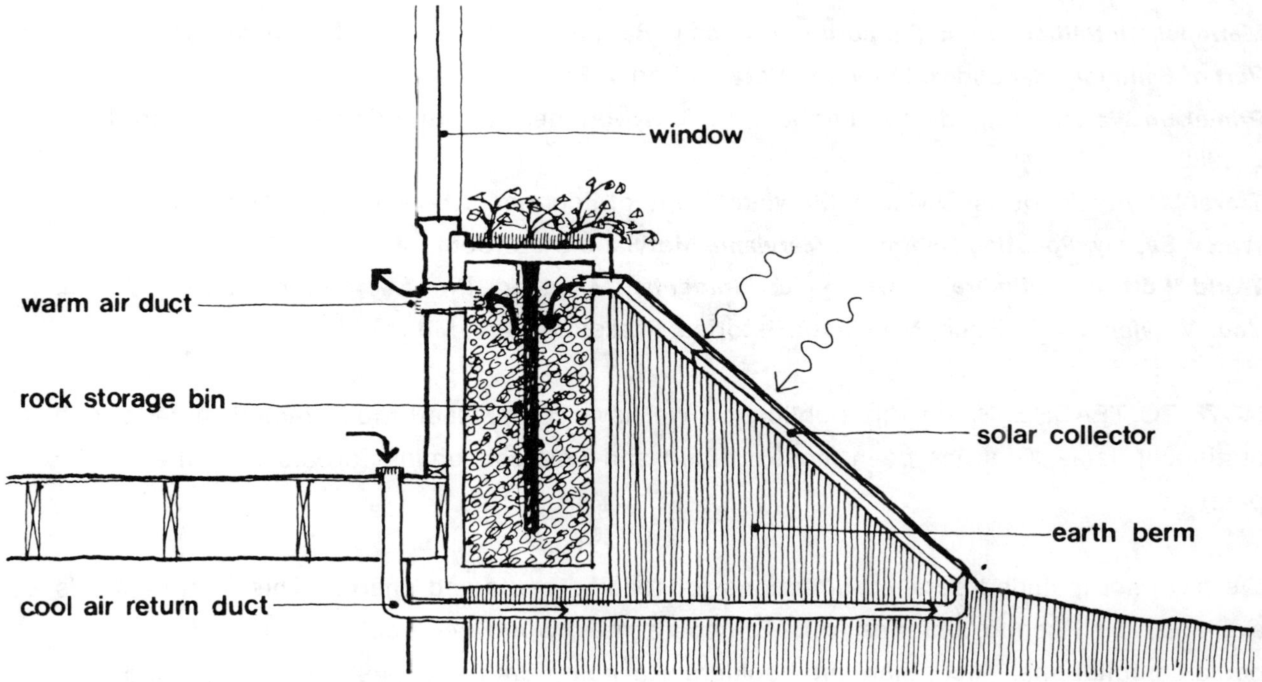

Solar collector units on earth berms (banked up soil).

From *Passive Design,* courtesy U.S.Dept. of Energy.

A LIST OF USEFUL BOOKS

Brief Industrial Facts (on each county and Baltimore City), Maryland Division of Economic Development. 1980.

Bureau of the Census, U. S. Dept. of Commerce, Maryland publications.

Economic and Social Atlas of Maryland, Department of Economic and Community Development Annapolis, Md.

Geography and Geology of Maryland, E. Vokes, Board of Natural Resources, 1961.

Geography of Maryland, Pearle Blood, Allyn and Bacon, Inc., 1964.

Maryland Economy, and the ***Maryland Economy and Maryland Projections Study,*** Research Division, Maryland Dept. of Economic Development, Annapolis, Md.

Maryland Forests, Craig Whitesell, Maryland Dept. of Education, Baltimore, Md. 1960.

Maryland Statistical Abstract, Maryland Dept. of Economic and Community Development, Annapolis, Md.

Maryland's Weather, Ashbaugh and Brancato, Board of Natural Resources, Annapolis, Md. 1961.

Maryland Wildlife, Maryland Game and Inland Fish Commission, Baltimore, Md.

Metropolitan Baltimore - Its Supporting Economy, Baltimore Association of Commerce.

Port of Baltimore Handbook, Maryland Port Authority, Baltimore, Md.

Primer on Water, Leopold and Langbein, U. S. Government Printing Office, Washington, D.C., 1960.

Travel Maryland, Tourist Division, Maryland Dept. of Economic Development, Annapolis, Md.

Water, Supply, Pollution Control: In Maryland, Maryland State Dept. of Health.

World Port of Baltimore, A Guide for Students, Maryland Port Authority, Baltimore, Md.

Your Maryland, V. F. Rollo, Maryland Historical Press, Lanham, Md.

NOTE TO TEACHERS: In this publication we have compressed much recent material and statistical data. This has been most difficult and time-consuming for you to gather in the past.

We have ***not*** included detailed directions for reading maps and charts. This information is available in all school libraries in U. S. geographies, world geographies, atlas and encyclopedia compilations. Also, there are booklets available from the publishers of these, and from manufacturers of maps and charts.

ACKNOWLEDGEMENT is due to many librarians, educators and Maryland State government personnel, for their kind assistance. The Maryland Department of Economic and Community Development, the Maryland Board of Natural Resources, the Tourist Division - State of Maryland, the U. S. Census Bureau, the Baltimore Association of Commerce and the Maryland Port Authority have rendered great assistance to the author. These persons and departments must be thanked every year or two again, since they evince continual expert guidance each time this geography is revised.

INDEX